The Economic Revolution

The Economic Revolution

Towards a sustainable future
by freeing the economy from money-making

by Willem Hoogendijk

International Books

International Books is an imprint
of publishing house Jan van Arkel,
Alexander Numankade 17, 3572 KP Utrecht, the Netherlands

© 1991/1993, by Willem Hoogendijk

Hoogendijk, Willem

The economic revolution : towards a sustainable future by
freeing the economy from money-making / by Willem
Hoogendijk : [ill.: Peter van der Vet ... et al]. - Utrecht :
Jan van Arkel – Ill.
ISBN 90-6224-997-3

Production: Trees Vulto DTP, Schalkwijk
Printed: Bariet, Ruinen
Illustrations: Peter van der Vet (unless stated otherwise)
Photographs: Kunsthistorisches Museum, Vienna;
                Ministry of Agriculture, The Hague

The cover is a reproduction of a painting by the Dutch artist
Friso ten Holt. It is one of the studies for his 'Children in the
Breakers' (1959). It is an image of people in the process of
liberation – hence the appearance on the book's cover. At
the same time, there is joy. And joyful revolutions should
be, or they should not be ...

"So, while it seems that there must be a limit to every form of wealth, in practice we find that the opposite occurs: all those engaged in acquiring goods go on increasing their coin without limit."

Aristotle

All evolution in thought and conduct
must at first appear as heresy and misconduct

George Bernard Shaw

Contents

Part One
Economics – an Attempt at Heresy

Part Two
The Liberating U-Turn

Part Three
Suggestions for Misconduct

Additions to the second printing
of the first edition

Summary

PART ONE – ECONOMICS – AN ATTEMPT AT HERESY

Contemporary production is negative. Just consider the destruction of the environment – the very basis of all production. Our (world)car is racing towards an abyss, and only a U-turn can save us. Every tap on the brake, every bit of slowing down and shrinking would be positive, would be ... real growth. The 'money-must-grow system', however, dictates continuous production, continuous (old-style) growth. It also gives rise to a narrow-minded, lop-sided kind of production, mainly of commodities that yield quick profits. Moreover, the negative 'spin-off' from this production – environmental degradation and human suffering – constantly creates new needs which we try in vain to repair with new production, that is by technical means. As a result, the path we are pursuing – although consisting of small steps, each logical in itself – is in fact an ever expanding spiral of misery.

PART TWO – THE LIBERATING U-TURN

Ways must be sought to liberate production from the grip of current finance, and its compulsion to growth, thus enabling entrepreneurs to act in a truly responsible manner. Employment should be organised more flexibly, separating it from the obligatory production of a single kind of good or service.
A two-track strategy is called for. On the one hand reduction, conversion or halting of the current, traditional mode of production. On the other, construction of a more intelligent form of economy, tuned more to basic than derived needs and building on the many alternative solutions already being practised all over the world.
By shrinking the economy, we could turn the spiral of misery into a spiral of progress, of real, durable progress.

PART THREE – SUGGESTIONS FOR MISCONDUCT

This part contains suggestions about what people, businesses, authorities and organisations can do to prepare for the Great U-turn. It goes without saying that these activities go beyond just furthering recycling and biking, or installing a filter on a factory chimney. Helping other people to develop a fresh view of economy and society is one of our primordial tasks.

Abbreviations
(For readers less familiar with English)

cfm.	in conformity/accordance with (a Dutch convention hereby launched in the global marketplace)
c.s.	and his/her circle (cum suis)
iou	a bond or promise to pay somebody (I owe you)
lp, cd, DA-tape	long-playing records, compact disks, digital audio tape (perhaps soon to be replaced by the competing DCC system)
mp	Member of Parliament
ngo's	Non-Governmental Organisations
vat	Value-Added Tax
vip	Very Important Person

Note

This book was produced with the help of the Institute of Environmental Education (SME), Utrecht, Netherlands. Financial support was obtained from the Dutch charities Earth and The Appletree. The illustrations were paid for partly with the environmental award of the city of Utrecht, which the author received in 1989.

Though not his mother tongue, the author has written in English so as to enable people in many countries to read it, not least in Eastern Europe where the Free Market now seems to be equated with Paradise.

The text was born as a paper for the 1990 conference on sustainable development in Bergen, Norway, and has been brushed up by Nigel Harle. It has gradually – in between other work – been extended to its present length, and shows the marks of these lop-sided growing pains.

Moreover, mainly in reaction to Herman Daly's last book (written with John Cobb), additionals points of discussion have been added as notes. A number of these might perhaps have been better incorporated in the main text. Some of the most urgent editing was carried out by Fern Morgan-Grenville. Nigel Harle did a last thorough check on the whole text. He also did the Index and was an inspiring support during the completion of the book.

As for the notes, they are longer than is normal practice in publishing land. In fact, they can be considered as a second, parallel text, enabling the reader to go through the main text unhindered by all sorts of additions and digressions.

Being an educator, the author uses a variety of images for society and the economy – a cart, an engine, a giant, a bus. PROMODECO has not succeeded in convincing him to stick to one metaphor. We therefore count on the reader's versatility...

It should be kept in mind that the author's viewpoint is that of an inhabitant of a 'rich' country with a fairly long democratic tradition and with reasonably reliable public institutions (government, army, police, justice). With 'our' countries the author therefore usually means these 'wealthier' ones.

For businessman, one should read businessman/woman.

The term 'productivism', adopted from the writings of the French sociologist and author André Gorz, will surely not meet with the approval of purists. It is used to indicate something ranging from an exclusive concern with production to 'production frenzy'.

Where the term 'natural resources' is used, we would often have preferred to add the wider term 'environmental functions', which includes the capacity of nature to replenish, store, purify, degrade, transport, replenish etc. (cfm. the Dutch economist Roefie Hueting).

Wherever it is stated that we should stop 'economic growth', it would have been more precise – but less common usage – to have said 'production growth'.

Please let us know of any questions or comments which may have been raised while reading this book.

Project Modern Economics (PROMODECO)
C/O SME
P.O. BOX 13030
3507 LA UTRECHT
NETHERLANDS

Preface

After completion of this text I came across 'Future Wealth – A new economics for the 21st century' by James Robertson (1990) – a treatise close to my thoughts. I was glad to find ample attention to the money system and the urge for public debate on this key issue. (I don't know whether I contributed in some small way to this development when in 1987 I met him and other supporters of 'The Other Economic Summit', an organisation with which Robertson was connected at the time. I had a paper on the subject: 'The money system and the system of interest', which was distributed within ECOROPA as well as at the GAIA Conference, Cornwall, 1987. Another incentive may well have been the publication of a booklet by the German 'Gesellian' Margrit Kennedy entitled 'Interest and inflation-free money'. See for my comments Note 34.)

Robertson deals with the required changes to the money system, transforming it into an effective and fair information system and a network of flows at the service of an 'enabling and conserving' economy. One of the many valuable parts of his book is the planning agenda for the nineties, with proposals for research and feasibility studies and for public discussion on various detailed subjects. I find this book a necessary complement to mine. In my book, the analysis of the current situation may be somewhat more thorough, which could help in avoiding naivety and in improving the strategy for change, but Robertson's book contains many valuable practical proposals.

While correcting this text, yet another book landed on my desk: 'For the Common Good – Redirecting the economy towards community, the environment and a sustainable future.' by the economist Herman Daly and the theologian John Cobb Jr., both from the USA. Since I refer to earlier writings by Daly, in several notes I have added references and provisional comments on his new book, which I could not study in full. It is again very commendable reading, with ample reference to traditional economic thinking and how this hinders change. The authors' proposals are broadly similar to my own (it's in the air, everywhere – albeit still mainly with minorities). They advocate a shift from individualism to a stance of person-in-community, from cosmopolitanism to communities-of-communities, from matter and rent to energy and biosphere. As for universities: a shift from academic discipline to thoughts of service to the community. As for economics: from chrematistics (money-making) to oikonomia. But Daly pays less attention than Robertson to the money system itself and in this respect (only) seems still to be the more traditional economist. His main line of thought does not seem to have altered since his earlier writings. The central thesis still remains: limits and restrictions at the macro-level, allowing freedom and dynamic competition at the micro-level. Both Protestants, Daly and Cobb stress the need for moral evolution in our societies, fostered by religious inspiration. Their numerous proposals for practical change in their country – the United States – make the book all the more valuable.

Both of these books see growth as something that we long for or are addicted to, and do indeed admit that the individual entrepreneur is compelled to grow in order to survive the pressures of competition. In neither of these two books, however, is it suggested that there might be a *general compulsion to production growth*, or that this compulsion is largely caused by the modern money system. This is not surprising, since my views on the subject are ignored and contested by most economists, including those in 'green' circles. *The suggestion and argumentation that the present money system causes a general compulsion to growth and the consequences of this link for the strategy of change form the subject of this book.* May its validity be weighed by further discussion and thought.

Thanks to comments by (mainly ECOROPA) readers of the draft text, I have added a 'Part III' with suggestions for concrete action on the part of individuals and groups. It was also suggested that I add an annotated list of 'alternative' projects to be found all over the world, but I prefer to prepare a new edition of my 'UTOPICS – a catalogue of alternatives' (1980, in Dutch only), if some money can be found. Throughout the text, enough existing 'alternatives' are mentioned to indicate the convivial contours of a new and intelligent society.

I feel confident that parts of the analysis, which has its roots in that elaborated from 1970 onwards by my old Dutch environmental pressure group Aktie Strohalm, will be new to many readers, and I consider this is the main value of this book. Without a proper analysis, that is, with an incomplete understanding of reality, our strategy for change will crash all too soon.

W.H.

Ill. Henk Groeneveld

Giant off-balance

"The difficulty lies, not in the new ideas, but in escaping from the old ones, which ramify, for those brought up as most of us have been, into every corner of our minds." (John Maynard Keynes)

The term 'sustainable development' has become common currency since the worldwide adoption of the United Nations report 'Our Common Future' on environment and development, the so-called Brundtland Report. The term is ambivalent. Many traditional politicians and businessmen welcome it. Some leaders translate it to 'sustainable growth'. Indeed, the Brundtland Commission itself advocates more economic growth in order to obtain the means to fight poverty, hunger and pollution – a catastrophic error, as I will endeavour to show.

As for the rich countries, I fear sustainable development will boil down to business-as-usual and, in addition, more or less selective growth. The true task in our present predicament, however, will be the *development of sustainability*.

This task necessarily involves stopping the dominant form of economic growth in the industrialised countries and achieving a severe cut in today's production volumes and a basic change in the nature of production. In a limited space (our ecosystem Earth), nothing can possibly grow indefinitely, unless one's aim is suicide. The choice, for the rich and the newly industrialised countries, now is: *to shrink or not to be.*

Against the background of ever increasing production volumes (use of energy and materials, of space and time, production of goods and services, etc.), measures like selective growth, energy-saving and recycling are dangerously insufficient and in fact misleading. Because they do not 'de-estrange' enough as regards the blatant craziness of the present production 'flood' (or indeed 'violence'), they generally represent a formidable obstacle to making people really aware of the necessity of the Great U-Turn, as Edward Goldsmith calls it.

In our current cultural context, however, everyone and everything has become dependent upon that growth. Our modern countries are like giants off-balance, compelled to run on in order not to fall. And, while running, they destroy trees, animals and landscapes. And water, air and soil. And villages, old town centres, proven social structures, people. Like Alice running in the looking-glass world, only taking her further away from her goal.

Modern economy – a giant off-balance, obliged to run on in order not to fall; destroying landscapes, animals, plants and towns...

Part One

Part One

Economics – an Attempt at Heresy

WHY GROWTH?

Approached from a historical angle, the growth of production, and the importance attached to it, are often traced back to the late Hellenic or Judaic-Christian cultures, Calvin, the Renaissance, Francis Bacon or the Enlightenment and their offshoots, including liberalism and socialism. Or to human nature. Or to technology (the Faustian Pursuit). Let us approach the subject in a more trivial, less cultural way.

If we intend to stop modern economic growth, because it appears to be fatal for the planet, we must first know whence it springs. We hear various reported locations of its source, but maybe the real source has still not been discovered, or is being concealed from us.

Where does this growth come from? Why such growth?

'Because there are so many people', so we have been taught. But we know that one million North Americans consume as much as about 20 million Chinese. And that the populations of most rich countries are falling while their Gross National Products keep on growing. Take note: this is not to argue against birth control, which is vital, but to bring into true perspective the population argument as applied to the developed countries, where it is often used to draw attention away from the role of industry and from the economy in general. In fact, each region of the world should in principle not foster more people than it can feed. (1)

'Our needs are without limits', so they have told us. But why all the advertising then, why all the pushing and cajoling to make us buy?

Entrepreneurs will tell us that competition and ever increasing

Development in the Netherlands

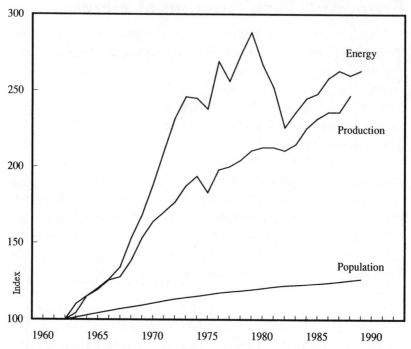

In industrialised and exporting countries, the relation between population on the one hand and production and energy on the other becomes ever more remote.

costs make it essential for them to grow; standing still would mean losing their market position and lead eventually to bankruptcy.

Municipalities want to grow, again because of rising costs; on top of this, more inhabitants and businesses mean more jobs, more income and more government subsidies. And the state, too, needs growth to meet rising costs and to pay interest on its loans, to support industry and agriculture and to be able to do more for its population, the environment, the Third World.

But are they really answers to the question: Why growth?

CONTINUOUS PRODUCTION

Let's look at production and its main source: business, i.e. factories, companies, corporations, farms, shops, retailers, workshops, etc., etc.

A naive-looking if not crazy question: *Why are businesses running continuously?* (I mean: every working day or round-the-clock and if possible at full capacity.) For a farm or a bread factory, continuous activity or production is normal: cows need to be milked every day and we need fresh bread daily. But a shoe factory? A car factory? Wouldn't it be more normal to slow down after the initial need for shoes or cars has been satisfied?

'It is for the sake of employment', the entrepreneur may answer. But why, then, that permanent process of automation, replacing people by machinery and chemical processes?

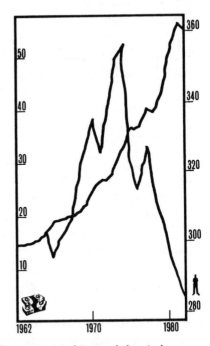

Turnover and employment at Unilever, from 1962. Machines and chemical processes have replaced human energy. The term 'labour productivity' (productivity per employee) to indicate the efficiency of a business loses its meaning and should be replaced by something like 'joule productivity'.

'Because' (another answer) 'I must ensure the continuity of the enterprise, providing income for the workers, the region, the state.' But if so, why the frequent closures of factories and transfer of production to other countries, countries with lower wages, less trade unionism, more lenient environmental standards and so on?

'Because' (a third answer) 'I must feed my investors – the sharehol-ders, the bank. Otherwise they will withdraw their money.'

HOW MONEY WORKS

The weightiest argument for continuous production appears to be: *because invested capital must be fed continuously.*

Capital accumulates. How? By putting one coin against another, thus producing a third, as is Nature's way? No. *Capital grows through production.* Money must 'work'.

Invested capital and loans increase through dividend or interest. Most of these returns are immediately reinvested in production, rather than used for consumption.

Why *interest?* Money, that means of exchange, has become a kind

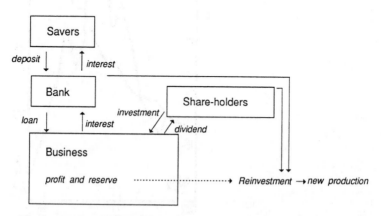

I. **The interest – profit relationship**
Because of the money-must-grow system, businesses are compelled to make a sur-plus profit – as well as a surplus reserve, in order to be able to survive competition, which is overheated by that same money system.

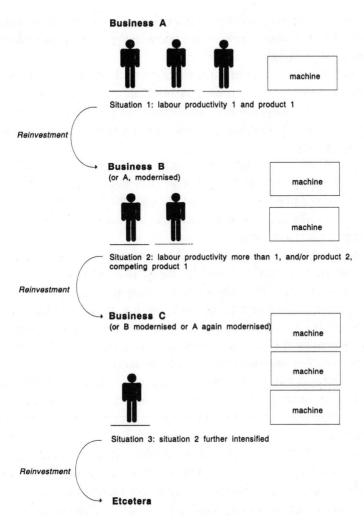

Business A

Situation 1: labour productivity 1 and product 1

Reinvestment

Business B
(or A, modernised)

Situation 2: labour productivity more than 1, and/or product 2, competing product 1

Reinvestment

Business C
(or B modernised or A again modernised)

Situation 3: situation 2 further intensified

Reinvestment

Etcetera

II. Reinvestment

With money not only from interest, dividend, profit or business reserve, but also from premiums and the like paid by and for the workforce into funds (for pensions, unemployment insurance, health care etc.), from rent paid for houses and land, and from many other sources.

of commodity with itself as its price. Interest has become an integral part of our financial lives. Yet various religions have forbidden or restricted it. Why?

The purpose or justification of interest is to remunerate people who save some of their money rather than spending it on consumer goods or otherwise. It is also considered to be remuneration for giving up part of one's liquidity, i.e. one's having ready cash to dispose of (cfm. Keynes).

However, rich people, rich companies or rich funds usually have enough money for consumption and are not in need of extra cash. They do not need to be lured into saving; they already have enough money to save (and, of course, all savings are invested). Or their very purpose is even to save.

It should also be remembered that today's money is to a large extent 'new money', created by banks lending money (providing credit) via current and loan accounts. Here again there is no sacrifice whatsoever on the part of the lender with regard to consumption or liquidity. (The only limitation is that imposed, for the purpose of guarantee, by the central or federal bank on the ratio between the banks' reserves and the amount they can lend.)

In fact, the whole 'institution of interest' boils down to little more than an automatic process of money being transferred from places of shortage to places of plenty. The result is accumulations of money.

Of course, pension funds have to feed their pensioners and banks their depositors. But they normally do this out of the returns on their invested capital, with part of these returns immediately being added to their capital (and reinvested). Again: accumulation.

Interest is a good instrument for keeping things going, to help new or 'renewing' entrepreneurs, to prevent money from being kept under the mattress, etc.

The entrepreneur or consumer in need of money will be glad to be able to borrow it. But they will have to work harder for it and the entrepreneur will probably raise the price of his/her product – for the consumer to pay.

In general, one can say: interest makes the rich richer and the big bigger – to the detriment of other people and things. And it forces up production.

Dividend – a certain part of a company's annual net profit paid to

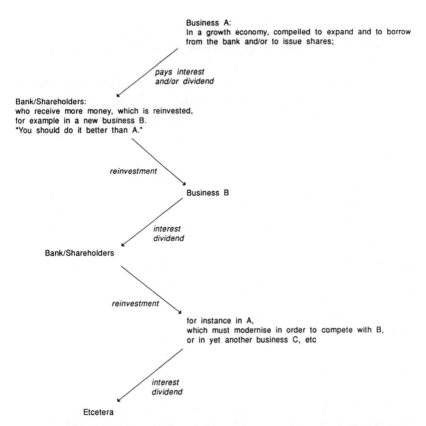

Business A:
In a growth economy, compelled to expand and to borrow from the bank and/or to issue shares;

pays interest and/or dividend

Bank/Shareholders:
who receive more money, which is reinvested, for example in a new business B.
"You should do it better than A."

reinvestment

Business B

interest dividend

Bank/Shareholders

reinvestment

for instance in A, which must modernise in order to compete with B, or in yet another business C, etc

interest dividend

Etcetera

III. The same process, in spiral

The money–must–grow system turns wholesome stimulation into hectic dynamism. Competition shifts from corrective to destructive.
Businesses that have to work with external money reinforce their own counterforces.

shareholders – is a less automatic institution, since it is a form of remuneration for financial investments that can be lost (risk capital). The business in which an investor takes a share may have bad years or even go bankrupt. In practice, though, dividends function as another powerful means of capital accumulation. And they oblige the entrepreneur to achieve extra production and profit.

And, lest we forget: although someone may lose his or her money, the money itself is not lost but will soon afterwards be added to another accumulation of capital and, from that new position, is reinvested and thus continues to drive up production.

In general, one could again say: dividend makes the rich richer and the big bigger – to the detriment of other people and things. And it forces up production. Interest, however, is the more automatic mechanism. (2)

Thus, an important source of money accumulation is profit-making – profits from trade, production and speculation. These profits are partly added to the capital of the business, and partly, in the case of shareholders, distributed in the form of a dividend. This source would not dry up if interest were minimised or abolished. (3)

Rich countries like Germany and Japan – and likewise rich individuals and businesses – have worked hard and earned a lot of money. (4) But beyond a certain point, this wealth has less to do with hard work or creativity and more with money accumulation having become automatic and exponential. (5)

MEANS OF POWER

Of course, money can be a good thing. It is a means of exchange, of overcoming barter, the useful 'joker' in the economic pack of cards, that does not perish like such old means of exchange as grain or cattle. It also serves as an indicator and regulator: those who make a profit on their products are apparently meeting important needs. A person who works hard is remunerated with money. Accumulations of money enable a country or a group of people to do things beyond the individual's capacity: building bridges, setting up a factory, founding a museum.

Money, however, has also become a *means of power* (moreover with a built-in, automatic mechanism for accumulation, as we have seen) which surpasses older means of power such as the slave chain, the possession of land or cattle, of an army or the corn depot. After all, a contract for employment or delivery or an IOU looks much nicer than a whip, doesn't it?

The money-must-grow system has in a way replaced the old system of class domination. Henry Ford is reported to have said that, if the people today understood the money system, there would be a revolution tomorrow. (6)

However, since someone who works hard or is cleverer than others earns more, the possession of (much) more money than one's neighbour is considered normal. Moreover, doesn't the state (the collective) correct this situation to a certain degree through income tax, death duties, etc.? So what's wrong with it? And anyway, haven't we all got some money in the bank on which we are keen to earn some interest? So again, what's wrong with it?

In old times, power was mainly linked to cattle or land. Power was limited to natural circumstances. With the introduction of money, however, power became more unattached. Capital is *mobile power*. With money, our era could break adrift. The workings and growth of money made us forget that nature has its limits – our second Fall...

'The money-lenders' by the Dutch painter Marinus van Roemerswaele (16th century).

"Just before the emergence of the great economic movements that gave birth to modern capitalism, medieval theology saved the usurer from Hell by inventing Purgatory. The usurer thus achieved his double aim: to preserve the Stock Exchange here on Earth without losing Eternal Life." (Jacques Le Goff, 'La bourse et la vie'.)

This process was greatly intensified by the coming of the steam engine and the increased use of fossil fuels, which enabled man to produce intensively almost anywhere and not only where there were slaves, timber, wind or water.

The steam engine is generally considered the cause of the explosion of growth in the 19th century. In fact, *the prime mover was capital*, which, having accumulated exponentially, turned workshops into manufactories and thence into factories. Bigger machines were required for spinning and other activities ... and those machines consequently needed more power than watermills and horses could provide.

EXCHANGE VALUE

Looking back beyond the Industrial Revolution, we see the process of financial 'colonisation' already occurring much earlier, in the form of accumulated capital (merchant houses, bankers, rich land owners), transforming traditional, regionally orientated agriculture into monocultural production of commodities for the national or international market: wool, flax, hops, later tulips, etc. The modern upscaling and intensification of agriculture, continuously requiring land reforms and the ousting of farmers from their homes, has ancient roots! (7)

In general, production for *exchange* has become the rule, to the detriment of production for meeting (normal) needs, for *use*. The exchange value of money has ousted its use value. Moreover, not only have products become commodities for the market, but also the means of production (cfm. Polanyi).

As for the development of the modern market, one does well to bear in mind that it 'deals' only in things whose value is expressed in money (hence excluding many important values and products of labour) and only with people who have enough money at their disposal to operate on the market.

DEPRECIATION

Another historical fact is the permanent depreciation of money.

In principle, the volume of money in use in a country should more or less be an expression of the total value of all goods and services in that country. The former should therefore remain in some balance with the latter. When the money volume increases more than goods and services, depreciation results. Hence grandpa's drink was 5 cents, your's 1 dollar. And his grandpa's drink was 1 cent.

Because of physical limits, the overall production volume cannot possibly keep pace with any sudden expansion of the amount of money in use and certainly not with today's expansion, mostly in the

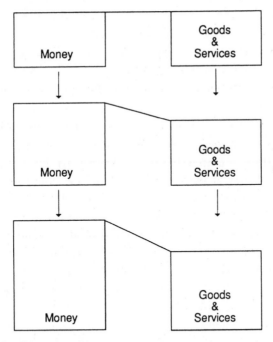

Depreciation of money
The volume of money should, in principle, remain in balance with the volume of goods and services. When the former increases more than the latter, money will lose some of its value. In particular, modern credit money has made the money volume grow – hence the continuous and rapid depreciation during the last century. Ongoing depreciation is one of the incentives for ongoing growth.

form of credit provided on account. Hence the *never-ending deprecia-tion of money* (not to be confused with the shorter-term fluctuations of inflation and deflation). This is one of the reasons that costs rise continuously and that governments are permanently faced with bud-get deficits.

Ongoing depreciation keeps the need for money permanently 'on edge'.

COMPETITION

The real problem is that *money drives up production* – and consequently distribution and consumption. How?

Financial returns are reinvested in new production, that is in new or existing businesses. In order to be successful in the market, to be competitive, investments can only be made in a new product or another version of an existing product – better, nicer, cheaper or just different: 'new'. These investments therefore call for and result in new or modernised production machines and processes, usually faster ones.

Confronted with this new competition from the market, other businesses are then also compelled to accelerate, modernise etc. – in fact even more so, for otherwise they will be pushed out of the market. (Hence their need to make extra profits and build up their own financial reserves.) In turn, this reaction must be answered by new, more competitive production ... and so on.

The result is an ongoing, accelerating and expanding *spiral of competition*, which has less to do with needs and usefulness than with money seeking to grow. An enterprise has to grow under penalty of disappearing. In the growth market, winners are 'over-winning', losers 'over-losing'. *The effect of competition changes from correction to destruction*.

The money-must-grow system is even more tragic or – if you are not yourself an ordinary, hard-working entrepreneur – curious, in that those working with outside capital (from shareholders or a bank) have to work harder (produce more, make more profit), in order to remunerate the investors/lenders. Thus they in fact help to augment capital that may well be reinvested in the very forms of production that will soon be competing with their own!

Competition usually also acts to lower the costs of production, i.e. the prices of energy, labour, raw materials and other natural resources. Poor workers and suppliers know all about it!

On the other hand, cheaper production, as a result of competition, means a lower price for the consumer. And surely, competition has other good effects, too? One does one's best, and bad entrepreneurs and products are pushed out of the market, thus improving customer service. A certain amount of dynamism, too, is welcome. Has it not contributed to better and cheaper goods, to amazing developments?

Take the old gramophone, then the LP, recently the CD, soon the

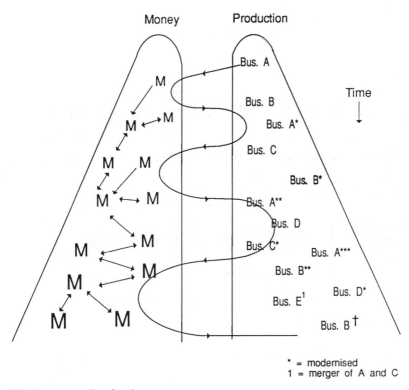

IV. Money → Production

The system of money-must-grow and competing capitals are the main factors behind the overheated competition between businesses.

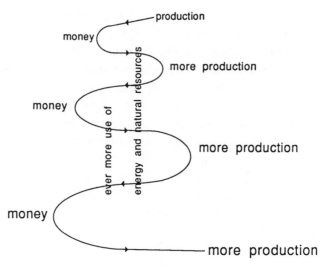

v. Spiral of Money → Production of goods and services
Ever more use of energy and natural resources

Vrijdag 15 januari 1988 | Boer e

RAI, BOEREN, BEDRIJVEN, BANKEN, INVESTERINGEN EN
wat banken te bieden hebben

Rabo, Amro, ABN vol verwachting naar de Rai

Boeren financieren
blijft aantrekkelijk

Translation: 'Dutch banks to agricultural trade fair with high hopes.
Financing farmers still attractive.'

Says a farmer from Groningen: "The whole economy is based on more and more
and bigger and bigger. The banks needle you the whole time. If things are going
well, they come and tell you you can expand again. 'Make sure you stay on the safe
side of the line. We can help you.' And before you know it, you're up to your
neck in new interest payments and instalments." (Hervormd Nederland, 6-8-83)

DA-tape or DCC cassette – isn't it marvellous? And all the cars, roads, shopping centres, super-trains, super-pigs, super-tomatoes, aeroplanes, clothes, cheap food from all over the world, holiday resorts. Not to forget all the rockets, starfighters and bombs...

'No', some people say, 'we're overdoing it. We've gone too far, much too far.' They are probably right and it is the money-must-grow system which is to blame.

On top of that, capital accumulation and the growing 'capitalisation' of production (production becoming ever more capital-intensive) lead to oligarchies and monopolies, despite state efforts to combat them by anti-trust legislation. The fact that in the shadow of these giants we see small workshops, boutiques etc. flowering and providing for some variety should not obscure our view of the overall scaling up and monopolizing of the main structures of production and distribution.

To resume, one could say that stocks of capital compete with one other by searching for the highest/quickest revenue through production (over and above all the numerous accumulation tricks practised within the financial world itself), thus forcing up production – and consequently distribution and consumption. (8)

The businessman's need for money is created by money's need for business.

NB. Of course, as a result of logical fluctuations in selling possibilities and natural bottlenecks, the path of continuous growth is necessarily paved with temporary recessions – upsetting, disturbing and causing more misery than pursuing the intelligent and controlled path of a planned total shrink and stabilisation.

MORE AND MORE

In this spiral of capital competition, the driving up of production has turned competition into counter-competition. *The advantages of competition no longer outweigh the destruction of capital goods,* i.e. the production machines that become obsolete faster and faster. The same wastage applies to many consumer goods. And think of all the waste resulting from all the parallel research and development work being done everywhere on the same kinds of product or model or process. (9)

Also, business today is primarily dependent on having access to money, rather than on producing quality or service or on being inventive.

The lower selling prices that often result from competition, oblige the producer to sell more in order to obtain the same turnover in money terms – another cause of production growth. Moreover, the turnover must usually increase every year for competitive reasons. It is common for managers to be instructed by their owners to achieve an annual increase of at least 10%. There is also competition with the rate of interest; if one can make, say, 10% on one's money at the bank or with bonds, production has to yield about the same in order to remain attractive for investors.

Competition, as developed under capitalist circumstances, has certainly brought forth very efficient systems at the level of the individual enterprises, but this efficiency relies crucially on sacrifices made at the macro-level and affecting nature, resources, social structures and the future.

The need for continued and ever more competitive production has led to a process characterised by 'more' – faster, bigger, flashier. At the same time though, despite the greater variety in many categories of consumer goods, it has led to an overall loss of diversity, i.e. the gradual loss of many labour-intensive services, goods and production methods.

'Overspeeding', 'oversizing', centralisation and continual mergers are some of the results. So are the vast numbers of new models, the creation of new 'needs' and the rapid changes in fashion in general. The reduction in quality that has accompanied the development of the throw-away philosophy forces us to replace our goods ever more quickly ('planned obsolescence'). It also increases the need for research (of a certain type, that is for market competition, to maintain the growth).

On the other hand, this spiral of production means that there are numerous things (goods and services, quality) which are no longer feasible to produce.

A dollar spent here cannot at the same time be used elsewhere; a

8000 sheets per hour

10,000 sheets per hour

One of the more hidden consequences of modern competition: the ever more
rapid, wasteful replacement of capital goods. A new production machine today is
outdated tomorrow.

barrel of oil used for this cannot be used for that. Thus, over-development has created and continues to create under-development. All
ongoing growth becomes 'overgrowth' – growth which surpasses
nature's carrying capacity. This is necessarily creating shortages, want.

The physical causes of this imbalance lie in the limits to nature's
carrying capacity and the delicate relationship between ordering (life)
and entropy. Nicholas Georgescu-Roegen, one of the first modern
economists to include entropy in his analysis, puts it this way: 'Every
time we produce a Cadillac, we irrevocably destroy an amount of low
entropy (= available energy and materials; w.h.) that could otherwise
be used for producing a plough or a spade.'

Our activities ought to remain within strict ecological limits. It is a misconception that modern technology allows us to extend them to any great extent.

ENTROPY

Entropy – the subject of physics' Second Law of Thermodynamics – is usually associated with disorder, an increase in entropy representing a loss of potential usefulness. Entropy is created whenever energy is transferred, some usable energy becoming unusable, for instance in the form of disappearing heat. Since everything can be considered as energy (matter, for instance, being stored energy), entropy is constantly being 'produced'. Iron turns into rust, a house into a ruin, order into disorder. The opposite is 'neg-entropy', from the ecological point of view the process of ordering on Earth, rooted ultimately in sunlight, through the process of photosynthesis. One could say that the whole 'trick' of life's evolution on Earth is to operate in such a way that there is just a bit more neg-entropy than entropy. All forms of life on Earth are the result of a (meagre but decisive) surplus gained on the entropy process. Life means resisting and deferring the degradation of energy.

The relation between energy and ordering is a delicate one. With everything we do, with everything we make, we produce entropy as well, as an inevitable by-product. Entropy we carry with us as our shadow. (10)

Wherever you ruin soil and plants, entropy accelerates again. Many deserts tell us where human civilisations went too far. An excessive energy input similarly disturbs the optimum resistance to

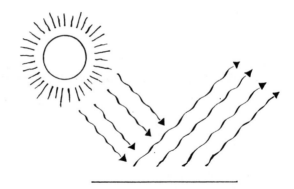

In a desert, almost full return (reflection) of sunlight, hence immediate loss of energy.

Through life and culture, sunlight is being captured and passed on, hence the delay of such losses.

The ordering of life on Earth can be defined as a process whereby nature (and limited human culture) builds up more and more resistance to energy 'degradation', succeeding better and better in preventing energy being degraded from useful to useless; or, stated differently: doing ever more with the same amount of energy.

energy decay, reached over millions of years. Such is the essence of the modern environmental catastrophe, accompanying the intensive use of fuels. *The essence is not a lack of energy, but too much.*

The whole Mediterranean area, where so many enjoy their holidays, is in fact an example of ancient erosion. All its surrounding regions and all its islands used to have enormous forests, full of animals. Too often, the legacy of human civilisations is ..... sand.
A hopeful addition: the maquis you find everywhere there (a valuable pioneer vegetation) is nature's way of trying to break up the rocks and make some soil again!

ECONOMICS OF NATURE

A few words about ecology and nature seem appropriate here.

Our eco-sphere is in fact just a very thin peel covering Earth's surface. Only within this thin layer is life possible. (11) It is based on photosynthesis, that miraculous process by which plants transform water, air and soil into basic organic material. This process is powered

Only in a very thin layer below and above the Earth's surface is life possible. This 'peel of life' looks immense, but is in fact very limited and vulnerable.

by sunlight. No wonder the ancients identified the four elements earth, water, air and fire as driving the life process. The energy of the sun is caught, stored and passed on, with the essential substances of life moving in cycles: water, carbon, oxygen, nitrogen and others. This highly complicated clockwork is kept going by the energy of the sun, which is expended, winding down from useful to useless as it flows through the system.

Our home. The Earth's crust is our floor, the ozone and other atmospheric layers form our roof, protecting us against heat and frost, poisonous materials and radiation from below and above. Carbon and radioactive and other toxic materials are stored safely away, enabling nature to develop as it has. Life itself has greatly contributed to this, and therefore to its own, development – the miracle of Gaia.
Man appeared and nature served him with a huge, rich larder. But he does not take proper care of this precious – and in fact his only real – 'capital'.

In this extremely complex network of organic and inorganic materials, everything is interlinked. The cutting of a forest may therefore well have effects thousands of miles away. The whole is more than the sum of the parts. This is the Miracle of Life!

The evolution of life on Earth can be characterised in terms of doing more and more, in an ever more varied way, with the same amount of energy, i.e. from the sun. (Nowadays, we do precisely the reverse by doing ever less with ever more energy...)

In the course of this evolution, our biosphere has undergone changes, both by the action of existing life-forms, and by enabling new life-forms to appear. Radioactivity has diminished, temperatures have become more moderate, humidity has increased. Metals and other materials have been stored away. Ultra-violet radiation has been filtered out. A lot of carbon was stocked away (outside the 'life-peel', now our fossil fuels) and, as a result, oxygen was freed – probably decisive for mammals!

Every new alteration permitted life to develop further. Man, the species, was one of the most recent life-forms to appear, which means that he is highly dependent on how the biosphere is constituted,

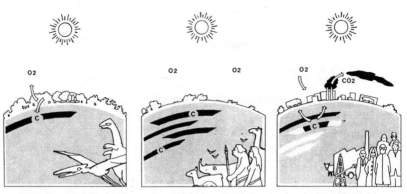

The process of storing carbon in the ground, putting more free oxygen into our 'peel of life' – mainly due to plants and allowing life to go on developing as it did – has been completely reversed by modern man. The same goes for the release of radioactivity, cadmium, mercury, etc. into the peel. And for the depletion of the ozone layer. Our present civilisation means suicide.

highly dependent on all the qualities that evolved at an earlier stage. Moreover, one does well to remember that Man is part of this complicated system, and that a part can never oversee or understand the whole – a truism which today we seem to ignore completely.

With this in mind, it is obvious that many current discussions are entirely beside the point. The question 'how far can we go with this or that alien substance?', the search for 'more proof that damage will occur if we continue polluting or warming up', or the retort that 'there is plenty of natural acidification caused by the sea, and Man's contribution is modest' are proofs of our ignorance. We are upsetting delicate balances. *We are reversing evolutionary processes completely, and nature will increasingly show the effects.*

The totality of life systems is more than the sum of its parts. That's why Life is so miraculous and, also, why environmental degradation turns out to be more catastrophic than we think...

Once we realise the enormity of this conclusion, we also become aware that discussions about how to supply the energy we need only show how alienated the participants are. Anyone with a better understanding of ecology and entropy knows that we already use much too much energy and will ask: 'What are our real needs?'. And, in the

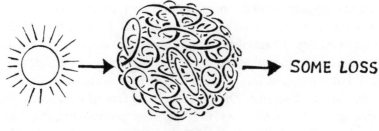

ECOSYSTEMS

In our biosphere, the materials essential for life move in cycles. The energy from the sun, which fuels this process, passes through the ecosystem, from useful (just used or even captured and passed on) to useless.

To switch to society, many people attach high hopes to the widespread recycling of materials, as opposed to the throw-away cult. We should, however, keep in mind that the speed of the cycles determines whether there is much or little need for, and loss of, energy. With regard to recycling, the point is again: we must do it calmly and within limits. The re-use of products, including packaging, is in most cases far better. Of course, the best option is to make only products we really need, and to make them last a long time.

wealthy countries: 'How do we achieve the necessary reduction in the overall volume of production? How do we get working on the Big Shrink, the drastic operation of Pruning Back?'

Finally inferring all this, we know that there is no choice but for 'deep ecology', as opposed to 'shallow environmentalism', for major changes and cut-backs in modern industry and for major reservations concerning 'ecological modernisation', because this will justify further (light-green) growth and 'business as usual'. (12)

So now we know how to answer engineers, politicians and the like who say that we can't put the clock back. In actual fact, this is exactly what they (we) have already done, and the whole job is now to get the clock running forward again properly – by means of changes that only their ignorance labels 'backward'!

Let's now get back to our economics and analyse its 'spiral' dynamics more closely.

LABOUR
ENERGY
MATERIALS
NATURE
WASTE

MONEY-ECONOMY

Similarly to ecosystems and the whole biosphere, the money economy is a circulating system. But contrary to the natural system, in which energy (the limited amount from the sun) circulates materials, in our economy it is the money that circulates, thus 'sucking in' and 'pulling through' labour, resources and fuel, land and nature. Moreover this is happening, ever faster and on an ever wider scale. The circulating part of the system is not a passive 'follower' being driven, but the driver, the prime mover.

THE SPIRAL OF MISERY

The process of: money → production (of goods and services) → more money → more production → etc. results in an ever expanding spiral which consumes ever more energy, natural resources, space and time. The initial results of this process were positive ('progress': production stayed within nature's carrying capacity). But because of its continuous character, it has turned negative and has now become a dramatic *spiral of misery*. This is ruining nature, which is, ironically, the very basis of production: soil, air, water, animals and plants which all form indispensable parts of our life-support system. As Herman Daly puts it, paraphrasing Adam Smith: 'The cardinal virtues of the past have become the cardinal sins of today.'

As far back as 1857, John Stuart Mill reminded us that the normal tendency of a natural system is first to grow and then to stabilise, and that societies would do well to do the same. For the same reason, surely you now eat less than when you were thirteen years old...

In ecological terms, one could also say that, after quantitative growth (the pioneer stage) comes qualitative growth (the climax stage: stabilisation). NB. I reluctantly use the word 'growth' here, in the light of what our present financial/economic system will continue to do with it ...

THE GAP

Misery? How come, when our Gross National Products always show an increase?

Well, it is now becoming common knowledge that our GNP's are not calculated in the most intelligent way. Our yardsticks are too short and we only apply them to activities that have a price tag: the countless non-market (e.g. household) and informal activities are left out.

Important costs such as those of environmental and health damage, as well as social costs and future costs, are neglected. Moreover, the activities with which we try to repair the damage caused by production are added on – thus creating a far too optimistic, and in fact misleading picture.

GNP measures production growth, not economic growth. The economy grows only if we succeed in satisfying more needs with the same scarce means. The GNP can therefore show an increase, while the economy is in decline.

To the open-minded analyst it will be clear that the result of our current overall 'production flow' is downright negative. Every day nature tries, through warnings and calamities, to sink this message deeper into our thick skulls.

One of the reasons the reductionist method of calculating has been so widely adopted is because of *the gap between business and society as a whole*. This gap is a direct heritage from past centuries and may well turn out to be a formidable obstacle to taking the measures necessary to clean up the environment, to slowing down and converting production, even to providing public information about production processes, product ingredients and their effects.

On the business side, this gap provides a freedom to operate and creates a feeling of detachment and unaccountability which we may no longer be able to afford – that is, if we are serious about saving mankind and the global ecosystem. (We must not close our eyes to the flaws of private enterprise under capitalist conditions just because the socialist economies have not been effective and did not succeed in producing enough consumer goods or food. A dirty Volga or Elbe doesn't clean the Thames, the Rhine or the Great Lakes in the USA! Nor, conversely, do dirty 'capitalist' waters justify rigid state bureaucracies, let alone one-party systems ... (13))

The gap was enlarged by the money system pushing its way into relationships which used to be directly linked. This process also had a disguising effect, because of the neutral appearance of money, contracts, etc. At the same time, of course, the money system has also furthered a more equitable relationship between people, substituting feudal links with relationships based on work and on exchange.

The gap between business and society at large is the reason that human labour is taxed far more heavily than fuel and other energy sources. The state needs this tax revenue to pay for social welfare, which has been brought more and more under its reponsibility and care.

The money system is also the main culprit in widening *the gap between the individual or family and society as a whole, the collective.*

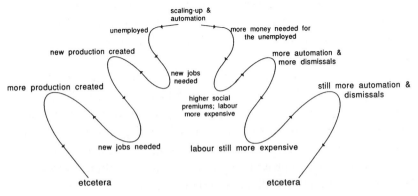

VI. Two spiralling results of automation and intensification
(in countries with well-developed social security systems)

Everyone becomes everyone else's competitor. Most people are 'prisoners' of the situation, as entrepreneurs or wage earners, and as consumers, inhabitants and parents. Every person and every business therefore operates according to what is best for him/her/itself, seeking (often obliged to seek) the biggest and/or quickest advantage. Taken together, however, all these logical activities of the individual parts are usually harmful to the whole, or may even destroy it: the *'tragedy of the commons'* (cfm. Garrett Hardin), the destruction of the common lands, currently of the world environment.

The 'victory' of the modern market has not only brought about the tragedy of the commons, but must also be held responsible for the present 'over-individualisation', indeed 'atomisation' of the populations of the rich countries.

Autumn 1987: Dutch fishermen clash with
government over catch limits.

The entrepreneur between money and nature

THE SUPPORTING CORK

As we have seen, the basic obstacle standing in the way of change is the dependence of everybody and everything on the present volume of production and the way it is organised (including the organisation of employment and the national income). It is the system of the *supporting base* – the profits from our market production (goods and services) paying for all public services and forming the cork on which we float.

The system of the 'supporting cork' means that production and trade provide the money the nation needs for collective expenses: for the economic infrastructure (roads, harbours, power etc.), education, health care, etc. An enormous increase in production – as has occurred in this century – generates much more public money, but the accompanying damage (ecological and social) also increases, even exponentially, i.e. explosively. This whole development may even produce an outright negative result. This obliges us to reconsider the entire system of the supporting cork. Shrinking production volumes may well mean: real progress!

How should we act, now that this base appears to be rotten, now that the result of that production turns out to be negative? Here we have reached the heart of the problem for our politicians and for ourselves: how do we slow down, prune back and convert our economy without overly upsetting our society, the people? (Upsetting will be unavoidable and even wholesome. I mean: without creating chaos.) To this end, it may be wise to form a still clearer idea of our present predicament.

In the early seventies, the Dutch artist Willem Holtrop (who lives in Paris) hit the nail on the head with his cartoon showing the fallacy of the idea that more economic growth was needed to cover the costs of fighting pollution.

HIERARCHY

Returning to our spiral of money → production → more money → etc., we observe a kind of hierarchy that is quite the opposite of what we have learned and are still being told about the factories producing in order to meet our needs.

Capital must grow and therefore, through investment, it compels factories to produce. So factories must produce and sell their products. And therefore the consumers, through shops which are compelled to sell, must buy: permanently and, because of the driving force of the money mechanism, to an increasing degree. And at all stages, the money suppliers are only too keen to help us by means of loans!

Since the consumer has limited 'swallowing capacity', there exist outlets for permanent production in the form of capital goods (production machines, airports, roads, laboratories, buildings – the whole economic infrastructure) which do not just require maintenance but are driven to constant modernisation.

As if this were not enough, there are also untold prestige projects in all shapes and sizes, and, last but not least, the armaments industries and the whole related field of space and other high-tech research.

This is the *hierarchy of money needing production, production needing selling, selling needing buying.*

Agreed, many people like to buy lots of things, preferably new things. Nevertheless, it seems more realistic to call ourselves *producer societies* rather than consumer societies – that over-used label that goes with the ideology of: 'The customer is always right', 'The factories work solely to serve us' and the like.

Admittedly, it's partly true that what consumers don't want will not be sold and will therefore eventually no longer be produced. But only to a certain extent, because business's whole machinery of persuasion (advertising, marketing) and planned obsolescence continuously work against this. Moreover, there are the increasingly important infrastructural and prestige outlets just mentioned and, finally, our needs are being determined more and more by structural reshaping (see below under 'Needs').

Consumer action and 'green consumerism' are valuable, but the idea that we can influence production through (non-)demand to any great degree is a common misunderstanding.

The Hierarchy of Compulsion

At all levels, capital is only too keen to help by means of investments, loans and consumer credits.

NB. The consumer is by no means the only outlet for production. The means of production themselves (machines, buildings, etc.), the continuous renewal of the entire economic infrastructure and products like weapons also play an important role.

EMANCIPATION

We are now in a position to understand more about *our recent history*. In order to sell, the factories (and the investments behind them) need consumers, i.e. people with money! Alongside the sincere desire to improve the conditions of the working class as industrialisation progressed, there grew a strong economic urge to provide money to a much greater part of the population than just the bourgeoisie. (14)

Although probably not by conscious design, one can still say that the advancement of our *working classes*, of the mass of our populations, and the rapid improvement of their living standards has been greatly furthered by the need for more sales and rentals: houses, bikes, radios, meat, furniture, clothes – to mention the major mass commodities in Europe between World Wars I and II. Moreover, more complicated techniques required better education. And, in general, a healthier and happier workforce does its job better.

VICTIMS

The growing production volumes of the 19th century had three victims: nature, the colonies and the working class (often jobless!) in our countries. In the rich countries, where the living standards of the masses have been considerably improved, at present only two victims remain: nature and the Third World countries, which are now in a way financial colonies. (15)

It is for this reason that the working class has become a firm ally of the present economic system and its production flood. Its struggle against the business owners has been reduced to a struggle for jobs and for better wages and working conditions. (16) The system as such is no longer questioned: labour's fundamental dependence on capital, indeed the reinforcement of dominating capital by that very labour. (17)

The next step in the process of 'progress' along this road of 'productivism' will of course be the similar advancement of the populations of the Second World (mainly Eastern Europe) and the Third World, again mainly through commodities. Quite understandably, most of them will welcome this. Nature, however, will not survive. In fact it may not even survive the burden currently being placed upon it by the rich and newly industrialised countries...

It may well be that big companies and multinationals will start to advocate a reversal of the present interest-on-debts stream from South to North. Production needs sales and hence purchasing power, as we have seen. So we can soon expect the pleas of Greens and 'Thirdworldists' for more help from North to South to be reinforced by business! (For a recent indication, see the appendix 'Outlines of the Nineties'.)

Back to history. So far, democratisation and emancipation have resulted less from a fairer division of the available cake than from an increase of that cake, at the expense of poor (made poor) countries and the source of all economic activities − nature. In this respect, the 20th century has not brought us much progress compared with the previous one.

Imagine what we will face when the cake cannot rise any more − or even has to diminish...

PSEUDO-SOLUTIONS

One of the results of the compulsion to produce commodities, which money generates, is the widespread belief in the *technical fix*, the technocratic ideology accompanying 'productivism'.

In this approach, problems are cut into pieces, into sub-problems, through the reductionist patterns of thought and forms of organisation which have become dominant, or 'natural'. For each of these pieces a technical solution is then sought, usually in the form of more production. Common-sense solutions which result in 'less', in slowing down or restricting or in abandonment are hardly ever considered. 'Productivism' wouldn't allow that!

Yet, for the simple reason that it not easy to create life or time, let alone highly complicated ecosystems, technical solutions are, almost by definition, inadequate and, by their consumption of energy, materials, science, people, environment and finance, harmful. Moreover, they make legitimate the usually fundamentally flawed situation they are trying to remedy. They normally boil down to *pseudo-solutions* that are more agreeable to the money-must-grow system than to our environment or our social structures. Politicians, too, are bound to these kinds of solutions, since they are also 'straitjacketed' by the short term and by the (growth) interests of their voters and the nation. In fact, more radical solutions will not even reach their windows.

These pseudo-solutions create new problems, which are again tackled with new pseudo-solutions, thus creating and enlarging the consuming, exploitative and exhausting spiral of misery. *Because we cannot master economic growth, states and corporations are developing biotechnology, nuclear power and a hundred other (often risky) 'life buoys' which are intended to allow us to keep growing.* However interesting, fascinating and challenging they may be, these techniques are being developed almost entirely because economic growth has gone completely out of control. And they will exacerbate this process still further.

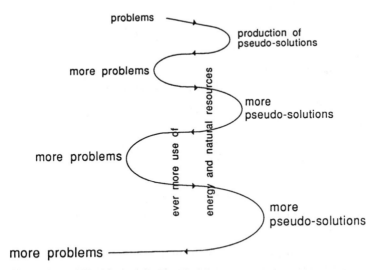

VII. Spiral of problems – pseudo-solutions
We tackle problems by isolating them from the wider context, in which many of their causes are to be found. Then we split them up into sub-problems (reductionist and short-term thinking) and try to remedy these with technical, usually end-of-the-pipe 'solutions'. For each solution a problem! New 'needs' come up continually.

TECHNOLOGY

We should also appreciate that different circumstances would have generated quite different kinds of technology. Ours is now based on the supposed abundance of energy and the supposed possibility of mastering nature. Imagine what could have been realised if 'developed' mankind had been less thrilled by Faustian engineers and had better understood the complexity of nature and the second law of thermodynamics, on entropy?!

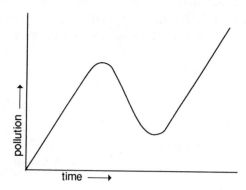

The so-called N-curve
Fighting pollution by technical means will, in the short run, result in some improvement. But in the long run it will appear just to have transferred the problems and consumed more energy and natural resources. After a while the general situation will have become worse. Result: an expanding spiral of misery.

The bourgeoisie, who adored growth, of course worshipped the first law of thermodynamics, the idea of energy never being lost, to the detriment of the second law about the inevitable loss of *usable* energy. This is similar to the bourgeoisie embracing Adam Smith's ideas about the self-interest-based market mechanism, while ignoring his warning that, without moral sentiments, a market economy would degenerate. (18)

It is not yet too late for a wiser technology, though. On the contrary, it would be an exciting development – provided we manage to avoid ongoing growth!

NEEDS

The expanding, self-reinforcing spiral of misery, driven by the lop-sided production of commodities and by pseudo-solutions, thus creates new problems and needs. The ancient Greek philospher Epicurus distinguished between needs (which are natural and necessary) and desires (which can be natural or unnatural).

Let me focus first on the *needs,* distinguishing four modern categories:

a. Basic needs ('natural and necessary'): food, clothes, shelter, love, sex, communication, work.
b. Needs for compensating past losses: for example, pools for learning to swim because the water our grandparents used to swim in has become too filthy, playgrounds because cars have now taken over our streets, etc.
c. Needs for repairing past damage: purification plants, the liming of acidified lakes and forests and so on and so forth – the realm of the booming eco-industry.
d. Needs created by past developments: for instance, the need for new jobs for those who have lost theirs as a result of automation; or the increased need for transport, through physical planning based on the geographical separation of functions (housing, work, recreation). (19)

Needless to say, the needs under b,c and d have increased enormously. In fact, most of the activities we and our society perform revolve around them. They form the compulsive activities generated by our 'prison': the production spiral. Since satisfaction or repairs are insufficient and normally leave the root cause of the need untouched, they stimulate the spiral by creating a continuous stream of new needs.

The spiral of needs → pseudo-repairs → new needs → etc., which again is the spiral of misery (usually labelled 'modern development', or 'progress'), consists of many smaller, interlinked spirals. They are all built up of small steps resulting logically from previous steps, from previous developments. However, the overall path we are thus following is fundamentally illogical and indeed catastrophic. The drama of the 'prisoners' who all, guided by individual or collective common sense (not so good for the 'commons'...), pave the way to self-destruction.

This analysis of needs again shows, by the way, that in the developed countries present-day production is related less to the number of people than to the level of technology and wealth and, above all, to the organisation of society and of production, distribution and consumption.

VIII. Spiral of misery

The development of modern society can be characterised as an attempt to solve problems, caused by production, by still more production. The result is a money-fueled 'spiral of misery', which consumes ever more energy, space, time and natural resources. This spiral is built up of numerous smaller and interlinked spirals, from all levels and sectors of the economy and society. Its parts are formed by millions of short-run, apparently logical everyday decisions on the part of businesses, political authorities and individuals – all prisoners of their situation. As a whole, though, the path we are thus following is **illogical** – disastrous in fact! Our task now is to start unwinding this catastrophic spiral – a hopeful path of real progress.

DESIRES

As indicated, besides this area of needs, there are also desires – the field
in which advertising and marketing people are all too keen to operate.
This field usually attracts greater criticism from environmentalists
than the structural creation of needs sketched above, which is more
important. (20)

Observing the individual consumers with their desires, the eager
(made eager) visitors to our modern shopping palaces, one realises that
they (we) are still partly hunters and gatherers. But they are certainly
also involved in the pursuit of compensation. The more we ourselves
are able to decide about our own lives, however, and able to influence
our jobs and the like, the less we will crave to surround ourselves with
the latest gadgets, the most fashionable clothes and so on. (Except, of
course, for the idle rich!) The more we can steer our lives, the less
important it becomes to hold on to the steering wheel of a flashy car...

Here again, class and education distinctions still play an important
role. (21)

THE UPSHOT

The various factors – money-must-grow, capital dominating labour,
the gap between society and business, reductionist science and calculation, and the atomisation of society: over-individualisation as opposed to a kind of what Ivan Illich calls 'conviviality' – together have
the following effects, a number of which have already been mentioned:

- The capitalist market economy has generated an enormous volume of production, which helped democracy to develop and
  which raised the standard of living. Discrimination and exploitation diminished, or became less visible, concealed by the money
  system which has a neutral appearance and also favours, apparently
  rightly, the stronger and the fitter.

- Competition has become ever less corrective and ever more destructive. It has become counter-productive: its basic advantages
  have been annihilated by the rapid destruction of products and
  machinery, of knowledge and optimally scaled networks, and by

the expulsion of numerous able entrepreneurs, craftsmen and workers from the market.

- Normal dynamism has become hectic productivity.
- Accessibility to capital has become more important than the ability to produce quality.
- There is continuous upscaling, inflation, intensification, acceleration.
- Optimum situations that have been reached are constantly being destroyed by the search for (more often: compulsion to) the *maximum*.
- Private interests dominate or constantly impede collective interests. There is a continuous tendency to privatise profits and socialise costs. Partial interests dominate larger interests.
- As many costs as possible are left out and passed on to new generations.
- Micro-efficiency, on the level of the business, is conflicting with macro-efficiency (at the level of the society).
- Production becomes increasingly capital-intensive (hence centralisation, mergers, etc.; this process is furthered by labour being surcharged far more heavily than energy). Labour-intensive production processes and services as well as smaller (normally sized) production units, shops etc. are forced out of business.
- There is continuous over-development, creating under-development elsewhere.
- Money is being continuously accumulated, thus making other people, sectors, regions, businesses, etc. poorer.
- Production for the market has become predominant, obstructing the satisfaction of other (often basic) needs.
- The short run dominates the long run, the present dominates the future. Short-term interests impede long-term interests.
- Education, science and research function to serve this system and its continuous, rudderless growth.
- Governments and other public authorities depend on the system's profits for their income. And out of the Treasury many important economic, social and cultural services are being paid...
- Our present economic system is not only destructive but also, because of its complexity and interdependence, highly vulnerable.

It holds everyone and everything in its grip, with no room for even the slightest hitch, under penalty of serious disruption.
• We suffer from severe alienation from the very mechanisms which rule our lives, our work, our societies, our economy.
• We are eroding Time, our Being. We are destroying our planet and all we hold dear.

In short, we are making ourselves pretty ridiculous by continuing to call ourselves 'homo sapiens'...

MONEY–MAKING

Let me call upon another ancient Greek philosopher, Aristotle. He argued with Plato, who was in favour of a kind of collective state, ruled by the best men, the 'aristoi' (who, by the way, were not supposed to be keen on money or status – truly aristoi therefore; something to remember for our new society...). Aristotle was more in favour of a kind of democracy.

As for economics, Aristotle clearly foresaw the cause of our present

"Very much disliked also is the practice of charging interest [tokismos]; and the dislike is fully justified, for the gain arises out of currency itself, not as a product of that for which currency was provided. Currency was intended to be a means of exchange, whereas interest represents an increase in the currency itself. Hence its name, for each animal produces its like [tokos = offspring], and interest is currency born of currency. And so of all types of business this is the most contrary to nature."
Aristotle, The Politics

plight. He distinguished between economics (oikonomia; the production for needs and exchange), trade and money-making (chrèmatistikè). He saw that trade for the sake of profit and the interest system lead to limitless money-making. Making money out of money is of all ways of obtaining possessions the most contrary to nature, he found.

If one's goal is no longer a 'satisfactory life' but 'life', one finds oneself on an insatiable path of 'ever more'. In this case, striving itself has become the goal, Aristotle explains – a process furthered by the use of money.

production for needs exchange (barter or through the intermediary of money)	natural
trade for monetary gain (for profit) [modern-times addition: production for profit]	unnatural
money lending against interest	the most contrary to nature

Aristotle's evaluation of economic activities

We would say, progress for progress' sake; the means dominating the ends. As regards his criticism of trade for profit, we would now add: and *production for profit* (i.e. producing solely in order to make a profit, as distinguished from an entrepreneur's normal reward. Admittedly, the modern businessman is *obliged* to make a substantial profit in order to keep up with the growth spiral, to stay alive in the rat race.)

With the rise of the money-making classes and powers – and our increasing alienation and, often, complicity – the wholesome and

---

Conversation

Q: How's the economy doing?

A: Well, uh ... uh ... holes in the ozone layer, above the North Pole too now. Nitrates in tap water. Genetic erosion. Global warming, with the prospect of rising sea levels. Acid rain. Deserts on the advance. Plants and animals dying out ...

Q: Wait a minute! I asked how the economy's doing?

A: Oh! Uh ... uh ... a lot of young people unemployed, women too, and men. Too many older people written off, too soon. For a lot of people, prospects aren't too good. Not much hope – people live from day to day. Standards are eroding, and the policy-makers are often the first to blame. Alienation from nature. Rich and poor countries with vulnerable monocultures – agricultural and industrial. Many people on the poverty line side by side with well-paid fellow citizens. A lot of famine in the world and massive debt in the developing countries. New epidemics on the rise. Drugs are spreading - chemical, recreational, ideolo...

Q: Sorry, but I asked you how the *economy* is doing?

A: Oh! Uh ... uh ... well, our balance of payments doesn't look too bad. The gas price is tight, though, because of oil prices. There are to be severe cut-backs in government spending. The national bank has reasonable reserves. Although some sectors of the economy are weak, others are showing definite growth with promising goods and services. Actual unemployment appears to be less than the statistics indicate. Overseas investments are on the rise. Thanks to this export of capital, the interest rate has climbed slightly. The investment climate here is improving. The OECD has issued warnings, but they always do.

Q: Thank you! That's what I wanted to know.

intelligent distinction between money-making and economy has all but disappeared. (22)

DICTATORSHIP

At present, the system of money-having-to-become-more-money (chrèmatistikè) exerts a kind of *silent dictatorship*, unrecognised as such: a totalitarian virus causing the productivist tumour which is destroying our Earth. (23)

The common concepts 'belief in growth', 'addiction to growth' and the like, are obscuring the underlying, compelling cause.

In countries with state capitalism, other means are used to boost productivity, like planning targets, sacking poor managers, etc. These countries, too, are in the grip of 'productivism'. The main motors behind this are the arms race, the struggle for power and prestige and the fight for raw materials, energy, markets, etc.

For a proper understanding of the matter, I should add that compulsive overstimulation through the money-must-grow system can occur anywhere money is introduced, whenever there is not enough community spirit (left) to tie money to its useful role as a means of exchange, and as a remunerator and regulator.

Money wants
to grow

People want
salaries

The State wants
tax money

Compulsion to Continued Production
Hence, Capital, Labour and the State all want factory chimneys to smoke continuously!

It is through money that the domination of castes, classes or tribes over one other can turn into capitalism. Conversely, capitalism and the associated kind of market economy can ruin the community spirit. Capitalism may be the cause of much evil, it is not necessarily always the root of it. It is part of a process of human communities or societies falling apart. (24)

Because states, governments and their policies and politicians are all subject to this system, with the same holding true for enterprises, banks, trade unions, etc., how can we stop the misery, the suicidal rush to the abyss?

Before going on to this, though, I must first add a few other observations; sorry, let's say to build up the suspense...

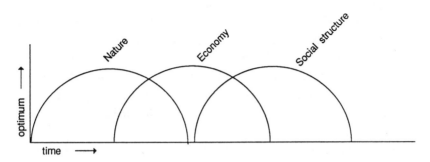

Human activity ('economy') is to the detriment of nature, and present-day economy, in turn, is to the detriment of social structures (communities, human-scale production, long-tried and optimum networks for making energy and materials last, etc.).

BEAUTY...

To understand our situation better, and the reason it is so difficult to adopt a different outlook, one should realise that to some extent the 'wrong' type of development has brought benefit to many and, also, that, to some extent, it is downright ....right!

Interest is to some extent useful (i.e. to encourage savings), and so is the accumulation of capital stocks. Some growth is good. To an extent, the flow of commodities serves to fulfil our basic needs. To an extent, competition is useful, for stimulating diligence, taming prices and weeding out bad businessmen and products. To an extent, the growth of trade and of the division of labour (= division of production) is an improvement. And so on.

...AND THE BEAST

The main problem is *the excess of it all.*

A development from 1 via 2 to 3 might be a good thing; continuation to 4, 5 and 6 may turn out to be negative. At some point, a flip-over point is reached. (Remember the virtues and sins Daly spoke of, and the development of ecosystems from the pioneer to the climax stage.)

The motto 'You can have too much of a good thing' should hang on every wall. As the French say: 'C'est le trop qui nuit.' Est modus in rebus (Horace) – one of the principal 'ecological essentials', to be brought (back) home to every human being.

It is fairly difficult to know where the flip-over point lies, because of our current frenzy of over-development and because we are all prisoners of this process. So we just carry on. When we also recall that this motor has always been used to develop and emancipate groups and classes of people previously lacking in opportunities, it becomes easier to understand why most people find it hard to grasp what's really going on.

The mixing of the various functions of money: as a means of exchange, of furthering activity and of accumulating power, was another development which has obscured our view.

Take an Engine (counter-arguments I)

Consider our society as a car engine. Money can serve as the lubricating oil that makes the engine run smoothly. It is also the fuel that keeps the engine running, with the speed being regulated by the gas pedal, the accelerator. (NB. It is not used up like real petrol, however, but flows back into the gas tank and thus keeps on circulating.) By means of the gas pedal – our collective powers of control and decision-making, as a country – the car can be driven fast or calmly. Because of the money-must-grow system and a too free market, however, money gets hold of the gas pedal and starts pressing it down itself. Hence, money becomes a dangerous driver or prime mover, and the car will take off on a blind and wild course.

Opponents of this analysis of money-driving-production will claim that the interest on a loan or on savings is covered by – and is a claim on – the future production that the loan will generate. In their view, money is driven by production.
They will also point out that the value of a country's currency is defined by the wealth and the installed production capacity of that country. If the country is devastated, its money will lose its value. So it has no value of its own.
In my view this does not contradict my point, though. Of course, if the car breaks down, the petrol will be of no more use. But as long as the car works it is fuelled by money, and the money-must-grow system may even get hold of the gas pedal and speed up the car, beyond our collective command and control.
The state, too, can speed up the car, i.e. by monetary injections.
However, if there is little to sell or to spend – as in the Soviet Union – the speed achieved will not be very high. People may have money, but there are no goods or services to spend it on.
So, indeed, in both economic systems there are physical limits to the extent money is able to drive the machine. The stage of economic development is important: has the country already embarked on the road of mass consumer goods, or is it still engaged mainly in producing capital goods? Has it already embarked on the spiral of pseudo-solutions and new needs, or is the economy still mainly geared to normal, basic needs? Power plays a role, too. More specifically, to what extent is the economy exploiting the Third World and Nature? The West has managed to turn itself into a Ferrari, the Soviet Union has got no further than the first Volkswagen...

Some circulation of money is fine, to make economic activities run smoothly and to overcome temporary stagnation. Too much and too rapid circulation, however, causes unnecessary and wasteful activities.

MIXED ECONOMY?

We should also bear in mind that the system of free enterprise, of a capitalist market economy, is in reality moderated by a wide variety of social and equalising laws, rules which protect the weaker (weakened) shoulders. (Before one forgets: partly the achievement of the socialist and other ethical movements!)

However, to speak of a 'mixed economy' – i.e. a mixture of collective planning and free enterprise – is probably too simplistic, and misjudges the strength of money and market imperatives. Before the collapse of the Iron Curtain and the whole 'perestroika' operation, Galbraith had already stated that the convergence of the planned economy and free market economy was underway. Such a development would, however, prerequire considerable 'perestroika' of the Western system as well...

Both state bureaucracy (state socialism, state capitalism) and corporate capitalism have eroded the more direct relations between people and furthered new class-like differences – the haves and have-nots, white collars and blue collars, those with a job and those unemployed, party members and others.

As for a planned economy, one should bear in mind that this does not necessarily require a one-party system. In a multi-party democracy, it is perfectly possible for the collective, through the elected parliament and government, to set limits on energy use, cars and so on and decide on the main areas of industrial investment, etc. Also, private property is perfectly compatible with a planned economy.

It might also be wise to recall that much social improvement in the 19th century must be credited to governmental (legal) guidance and state interference, correcting an all too enthusiastic dynamics of 'laisser-faire'. (25)

MITSHULEVER LTD.

Because of the money-must-grow system, accumulation of capital stocks goes on and on (despite anti-trust laws!). Every day we read about business mergers, take-overs and the like. We're surely destined to end up being 'governed' by huge transnational corporations named Espont and Mitshulever.

The word *'supern*ational' may be more in accordance with reality than *'trans*national' or *'multi*national' – hence the word 'governed'. But I should add that in my analysis, even transnationals have limited freedom of operation, again because of the money system, because investments (shareholders) require constant feeding. And the entire competitive system forms a kind of prison. (26) However, multinational corporations as well as banks are the instruments 'par excellence' for capital accumulation. It is money-making (chrèmatistikè) which pushes the development of armaments, drugs, artificial fertilisers, pesticides, medicaments, oil consumption, electronic devices, biotechnology, the car system, etc.

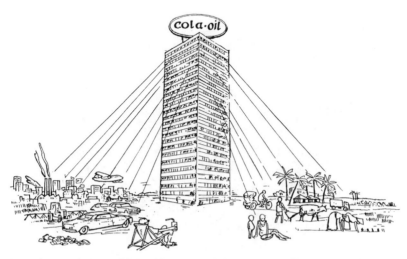

Sure, the populations of the rich countries (left) are better off than those of the other countries (right). Sure, the richness of the former is the poverty of the rest. But the ruling power structure (Big Money plus Technology) is the same for both.

This process of accumulation is the reason for the disappearance of so many small trades, shops and factories (having become small because of the growth of others!) and of old, often efficient structures, lines and networks, representing variety, quality and service. The constant flow of money from small to big accumulations has filled the world with dazzling commodities and huge-scaled structures, while at the same time causing impoverishment (including cultural impoverishment) to which the dazzle has regrettably made us blind.

And the process goes so fast! What do our children today know of our parents' world? Here again we find a serious cause of overall alienation.

Another lies in the fact that our civilisations have become increasingly urbanised, and thus estranged from the land (except as an object for financial colonisation!), from agriculture, from the essential natural processes and the animal and human labour that provide our daily food, our clothes, etc. Whereas in fact the whole world keeps on turning and all our economies keep on turning only because all over the world there are millions of people doing their daily work – the kind of work which many estranged and spoiled 'white collars' and 'arti's' would call 'dull'...

Although Man's dependence on other people has increased enormously in modern times, his or her awareness of this has diminished at an equal rate. Our individualisation goes hand in hand with our alienation.

THE MONEY CLOUD

Just before assuming office, the president of the International Monetary Fund, Michel Camdessus, drew attention to the gap between the world of finance and the world of production, which he found worrying. He spoke of: '...the enormous weight of a proliferative financial sector that covers with its shadow the real economy and threatens to suffocate it.' (27)

It is estimated that the money circulating in the financial world itself is some 30 times greater than that circulating in the realm of production (the real economy, as Camdessus says). It seems wise to consider that world more or less as a parasite upon production and upon society as a whole.

Moreover, a huge cloud of free money is hanging over the world, moving unpredictably, influencing at random: today buying dollars, tomorrow yens or marks. Or other values. (28)

As for financial power and the hidden character of the money-must-grow system, we may recall that, in former centuries, the European countries (and the companies seated there) were the mightiest financial powers in the world (Venice, Spain, later Holland and Britain). Around 1900 the USA took over this leading role. Today, Japan apparently holds this place. Perhaps, as those 'very alien' Japanese have now become the main global 'financial colonisers', the leading classes in Europe and North America, in their gradual transformation from exploiters to exploited, will at last discover how the money system really works! (Unless their high salaries and other incomes keep on standing in the way of this revelation.)

THE STATE

The state has already been mentioned a few times. It used to be pictured as a kind of neutral arbiter between Labour and Capital, the traditional antagonism. But the state is in fact heavily dependent on the market economy for its income and is therefore more the servant of the mightier of the two – Capital – than of Labour, or let us say, of the population in general and of the public interest. Hence its present difficulty, for instance, in defending the environment against short-term economic interests and developments.

According to the idea that production serves as its supporting base (the cork), the nation state is usually considered to be a big spender. Whereas one could in fact also regard it as a producer, namely a producer of the whole economic infrastructure and of education, welfare, justice, health care, security, etc. These are useful things,

Concentrations of capital within countries

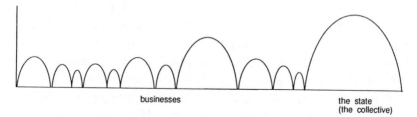

businesses   the state
                                                        (the collective)

I. **Corporate capitalism or the modern, 'mixed' economy**
Situation in most industrialised countries.
Businesses, funds and banks are increasingly part of transnationally organised capital.

Tendency towards further concentration (see ill. II). (This led the U.S. consumer-interest defender Ralph Nader to use the accusing term 'concern-socialism'!)
Some corporations dispose of more money than medium-sized nations.
As regards the state, the collective: there is little 'free' money. Most expenditure is fixed: public services such as education, health care, defence, economic infrastructure, housing, and interest on the national debt.
NB. The less socially and ecologically businesses behave (or are compelled to behave in order to survive overheated competition), the more it is the state that must regulate.

surely, though this is also a development which has made the business world, the world of private production as free and unimpeded as it presently is. (One could also say: unconcerned, not very socially-minded.)

A short-term problem confronting many nations is their growing debt burden. New public loans are increasingly being used to pay the interest on the previous loans. A strangling spiral. Is it preluding something worse?

All our states currently suffer from a lack of money. Why? As pointed out, there is the general depreciation of money and a consequent rising of costs, and business can cope with this faster than can governments. But there may be more reasons. Banks and companies make huge profits and need to do so because of the ever harsher competition and the constant upscaling it gives rise to. Could it be that the devouring competition between the big enterprises requires

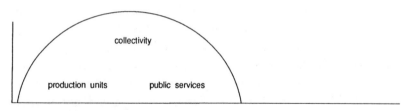

II. State socialism or state capitalism
Comment unnecessary ...

III. More equalised economy or 'free' economy
As many people as possible can participate as independent producers or equal members of productive groups or as well-treated and participating employees – of course regulated by general ecotaxing, anti-trust legislation etc.

NB. The followers of Silvio Gesell call it a 'free economy' (Freie Wirtschaft), but I hesitate to adopt this term in view of the enormous restrictions we have to impose on ourselves in order to balance our activities with nature's carrying capacity.

so much money, causing such an immense money drain, that states will increasingly face financial shortages and may even eventually go bankrupt – even the ones which are now rich?

EASTERN EUROPE

Criticism of the economies and pollution in the Eastern European countries is not as fully justified as it seems.

Let's see – how was the situation when the countries of North-West Europe made their change from agricultural to industrial nations, in the 19th century? Priority was given to the production of capital goods: ships, trains, production machines. Many people lived in poor houses. There were very few consumer goods. The pollution was considerable and the hygiene bad. Workers' organisations were opposed.

Eastern Europe experienced this change to (further) industrialisation during this century and at an accelerated pace, while Russia made additional efforts to produce armaments (World War II, the Arms Race) and carry out space projects (for military and status purposes). (29) Part of the tragedy has been the existence of developed consumerism westward – and the magnetism it exerted with which the working class of 19th century Western Europe did not have to contend.

What would have been the situation in the Eastern European countries if, after World War II, they had lived under the same free conditions as the West? Well, they would not have been very different from Denmark, Ireland or Belgium – depending on their particular rate of industrialisation. As in Western Europe, pollution would have been less visible than now, more diluted or exported (to poorer countries...). The use of energy and raw materials would have been more efficient but much greater. There would have been far more car traffic (impeding public transport and demolishing cities), much greater use of artificial fertilisers and imported animal fodder, and other Western 'mistakes'. Much more import and export. Many (too many?) consumer goods.

Certainly, the standard of living would have become higher, based on much greater exploitation of nature and the Third World – as has been the case in the Western European countries and the other rich Northern countries. Discrimination would have been exerted, not by an elite party but (probably more tolerably) through the money system, by the accumulation of capital. People would have been dependent on capital instead of on bureaucratic decisions.

A more tragic scenario could have been – and is still possible for Eastern European countries! – their becoming a kind of colonies for the rich countries, or becoming neglected areas, only good for providing cheap labour, like southern Italy in comparison with northern Italy. (For the polarity of over- and underdevelopment, see Appendix 1 'From Sandy Soils to the Sahel'.)

At present, following their liberation from the one-party system and economic state bureaucracy, these countries have high expectations of the Free Market system. I am afraid they will start off by making many of the same mistakes which the free-market countries have made and are still relentlessly making. And I am afraid one has to accept that this will happen. Only nature and the Third World will suffer, and they have no voice, no power...

Western and Japanese capital will now eagerly 'civiloit' (civilise and exploit) Eastern Europe – and continue to do so in ever larger parts of the Third World. *Nature will not be able to cope with the increased pressure of this ongoing 'productivism'.*

But let us now at last turn to solutions. (Though I may add some more pieces of analysis where necessary. The reader should not forget how strongly our current approach to things has blinded us, and will therefore hopefully forgive me...)

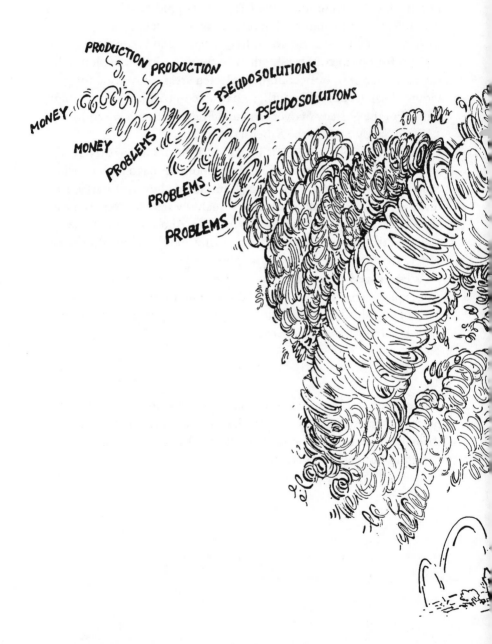

Part Two

The Liberating U-Turn

'The time has come to break out of past patterns. Attempts to maintain social and ecological stability through old approaches to development and environmental protection will increase instability. Security must be sought through change.' (U.N. report *'Our Common Future'*)

The picture of our society we sketched in the first part was of a giant off-balance who has to run on in order not to fall. (30) We might also liken it to a bus in which we are all sitting and which is racing towards an abyss. The driver and the passengers now know that the speed and the road may not be in order, but they (we) nevertheless go on chatting, reading and listening to music. Society (the bus) goes on. We work, do business as usual and go on holiday. We sit in the pub, frequent fitness centres and so on.

A bus racing towards the abyss. Therefore, every tap on the brake, even a weak one, is a wholesome activity, is positive, is...growth!

Our main task now is to get that bus to stop and make a complete U-turn (cfm. Edward Goldsmith, Otto Ullrich and many others).

The Great U-Turn is absolutely essential. It is also not as worrying or strange as it may appear, because modern mankind has already made a great U-turn in the evolution of the Earth, particularly by releasing the carbon and other substances stored over millennia. Therefore, the U-turn advocated here is really only a *correction* of the very stupid turn which we (the developed countries) made in earlier years.

How do we make that corrective U-turn?

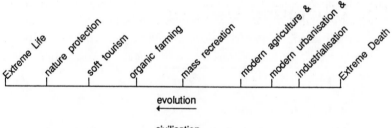

This scale shows the degree of degradation of nature (i.e. the basis of human economy) through human activities (cfm. Pieter Schroevers).
One could say that natural evolution moves from extreme death to extreme life, whereas human civilisations have, up to now, moved in the other direction.
Some people think that a society can choose where to situate itself on this scale. That is to say: a modest level of production and a frugal lifestyle with plenty of nature, or more production and wealth with less nature. For stabilised, self-controlled economies it should indeed be possible to make such a choice. However, the uncontrolled growth economies that 'developed' humans seem to have been unable to avoid so far, slide inevitably towards Extreme Death.

POSITIVE DEVELOPMENTS

Some encouraging developments:
- The many proposals elaborated by environmentalists, such as eco-taxing, i.e. making labour cheaper and energy, materials, natural resources etc. more expensive; cheap capital for eco-projects; reduction of production volumes; 'soft' technology, renewable energy and so on; the discussion about a basic income and similar forms of social innovation.
- The numerous alternative solutions already developed, usually by ordinary, ecologically and socially conscious citizens – all over the world, in many sectors of society. Alternatives as answers to the official solutions which worked out wrong, fell to pieces or grew too expensive. (31)
Proven alternatives range from an old people's home that has set up a small farm, and a municipality managing to tame car traffic, to

organic farms. Or from the installation of a battery of wind turbines, and inhabitants of a town district who managed to decide on how their district was to develop, to a bank that works with lower interest rates, and communities which have set up their own system of exchange. (32)

Other encouraging developments:
- The growing ecological awareness among consumers.
- The growing ecological awareness among politicians, civil servants, businessmen, trade unionists, etc.
- People being generally better informed, thanks to the modern media, environmental education and the slow emergence of a one-world awareness.
- The increasing interest in human relations, non-material values, spirituality and the old values of religions and philosophies of life.
- Oddly enough: the many jobless and discarded (or almost discarded) labourers, women and craftsmen, shopkeepers, farmers and (other) businessmen. Admittedly, most of them want a regular job in the present economy, but could they not become a vital, because available, force in the new economy? And what about the present waste of keeping or making useless so many young and old people?
- The emergence of a feminine world, more life-oriented and Earth-bound and usually with a more common-sense approach to people and things.
- The progressive parts of the Third World (excluding the elites who just wish to rule and enjoy wealth).
- The diminishing importance of the arms race, at least between the superpowers, which could free money, science and materials for clean technology, for regreening the planet, etc.

This list also shows where we can find our *allies* for the U-turn.

THE SPIRAL OF PROGRESS

Another important positive element is the probability that, once we make the U-turn (the Germans say 'umdenken und umtun') and start unwinding that spiral of misery by reversing all the current trends, we may well find that the results are more numerous than anticipated. This is a kind of positive mirror image of the ever more disappointing results experienced when the spiral was formed, when we applied our inadequate technical pseudo-solutions, which in turn continually required new remedies.

Some examples: bringing housing, working and recreation closer together will not only decrease our need for transport, but also diminish our burden on space and the landscape. More work in the garden and more community work will mean more TV sets switched off. Eating less meat and fat will mean healthier people. Cosier and cleaner cities will mean less need for, and pressure on, recreational facilities elsewhere. More society-oriented education will stimulate learning results. More jobs and work will diminish boredom and vandalism (cfm. 'eco-city' Davis, 33).

To avoid any misunderstanding: I here mean just the concomitant effects, the 'spin-off' of the positive spiral which comes on top of the enormous direct advantages of the U-turning operations – reducing volumes, taming the car system, saving proteins and energy, converting industry, applying soft and clean techniques, and so on – in terms of their effects on the environment, on employment and community, on time and space.

The happy opposite of the spiral of misery is the *spiral of progress*!

TAMING MONEY

In former times, the main controversy or conflict in society was between the working class (the factor Labour) and the bourgeoisie (the factor Capital). Nowadays, this controversy has apparently calmed down because capitalism has helped to improve general welfare and the labour factor now embraces it. In future, I anticipate, we will witness a further transformation of the old antagonism, in that *the vast majority of the population (including open-minded, 'de-hooked' managers, bankers, etc.) will come to appreciate the true functioning of the money-must-grow system and try to free themselves from it or to tame it.* (34)

With liberalism these days triumphing everywhere over socialism, some people, like Frances Fukuyama, are talking about the end of

Which wallpaper is really modern?

history. But history is only just beginning! Mankind has still to free itself from – metaphorically speaking – 'pre-historic' features and structures!

Liberalism now means 'liberal capitalism': making way for capital and, surely, giving more chances to more people. But both these advantages are always to the detriment of other people and countries, of future generations and nature. This liberalism is the ideology of production-centred, money-accumulating capitalism.

In fact, the world of capital and big business had better change its tune. Its pretensions are really hilarious if one only considers
- to what extent the state pays for the economic infrastructure,
- how health, environmental and social expenses are passed on to other regions and future generations,
- the number of investment premiums, grants and tax facilities it receives out of the collective purse, including development aid which is often to be spent in the donor countries.
(Not to mention all the other collective expenses discussed earlier, which have 'desocialised' production.)

Some people point out that 'selective growth' could mean less coal, more wind power, fewer cars, more books, fewer weapons, more concerts, fewer foreign holidays, more camping in one's own country, etc. I am not at all against such a development, but would point out that capital can and does also accumulate by means of 'green' products, cultural goods and services and the like – in fact, in all activities in which money ('power capital' that is, big money) is involved. So let's not forget to change not only the products but also the overall context, taking into consideration growth incentives, control, general direction of investments, power in the realm of information and so on.

SOME FIGURES

Before we come to outlining a strategy for change, let me attempt to translate into figures (merely tentatively!) the result of the Great U-Turn, the Great Prune-back.

Let us take the present revenue of the economy of a so-called developed nation as 100. As we have seen, the greater part of that amount is spent on repairing the damage caused by generating the revenue, on compensating for past losses, and on financing 'system-generated' needs (i.e. the needs b, c and d mentioned in Part I). Let's assume these cost 60, which leaves a net result of 40.

	Gross		Repair compensation etc.		Net result	
Now	100	—	60	=	40	
		Shrink of 60%				Step back of 25%
Future	40	—	10	=	30	

The unwinding of the spiral of misery will not be as catastrophic as it might first appear. A shrinkage of as much as 60% may well result in a far smaller reduction in net result (say, 25%), because the costs for repair, compensation, etc. will be considerably lower. Many environmentalists and 'green' economists estimate that the result of modern economies has already become downright negative (for repair, compensation, etc. say, 150%), so that any shrinking is pure gain.

A different economy – cleaner, much calmer, more intelligent, i.e. with less waste, luxury, Cadillacs, etc. – might well produce only 40 as its gross product. However, the item 'repair, etc.' would then amount to only 10, which makes the net result 30.

If we now compare the old result of 40 and the new one of 30, we find a true regression of only 10! The resulting figure of 30 may well correspond to what our level of wealth was in around 1960, which is not at all 'retrograde' but, on the contrary, very wealthy. The Big Shrink would leave enough 'cake' to share (more equally). There would be plenty of scope for useful scientific research, too, for instance.

Today, however, one would be declared absolutely insane if one dared to advocate, for the rich countries, a 60% decrease in production!

In my view, the picture of the Big Shrink is even rosier in reality, in that the present economy is downright negative (the bus racing towards the abyss; hence repair 150!) so that any other economy, any calming down, means gain. (35)

TWO-TRACK STRATEGY

In the u.n. report 'Our Common Future', the 'Brundtland Report' – which unfortunately relies on the traditional growth imperative – we read that the only possible solution is through *change*. The 'bold, imaginative leap forward', in the words of Prince Charles.

The main *strategy* for such a change in our countries should now be a *two-track* one.

With one hand we should apply an axe to the overscaled, compulsive production system with its worldwide 'overtrade'. With the other we should build up a normally scaled, more self-sufficient, 'green' economy, helped by the alternative, trend-setting solutions already existing everywhere.

This operation should be a twinned one, like communicating vessels, one downwards, the other upwards. Ecological limits definitely do not permit us simply to add wind turbines and so on to current production volumes. We must shrink the economy. Therefore, the room for soft new technologies should be provided by first stopping all unnecessary activities. (36)

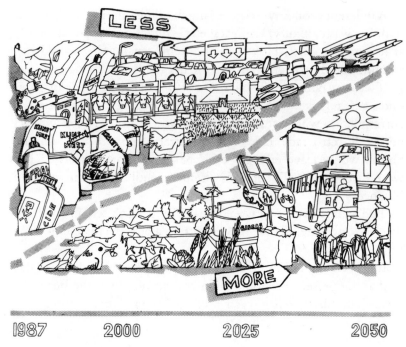

Two-track strategy of slowing/stopping and development. The total result should, however, not be further economic growth, however selective or 'green', but a Big Shrink, in terms of the use of energy, materials, space and nature. The joyful spiral of progress!

Part of the twin-track operation will of course consist of maintaining or converting the many valuable and suitable parts of existing industrial equipment and technology. However, if we do not make a clean break from past trends, it will, I repeat, be business as usual, at best only slightly more selective. The bus will still head for the abyss, but at a slightly slower speed. Desperate diseases require desperate remedies, so runaway vehicles require strong braking.

There is perhaps hope in recalling the drastic change a country like Britain had to make when it declared war on Hitler's Germany in 1939, being obliged to change from a peacetime to a wartime economy almost overnight.

The U-turn now needed would require a fighting spirit not merely for 6 years but for, say, 60 years. Ending, let's hope, in a lasting attitude of care for the ecosystem Earth and the human community. It will require 'guts, sweat and tears' – to paraphrase Winston Churchill – and the reward will 'only' be more healthy and tasteful fish-and-chips...

INFORMATION

Needless to say, this drastic operation should be preluded and accompanied by a *vast campaign of information and education* (again, in accordance with the U.N. report 'Our Common Future': 'The changes in attitudes, in social values and in aspirations that the report urges will depend on vast campaigns of education, debate and public participation.'). Such a campaign should use all communication media, schools and training programmes and aim at full citizens' participation. The foundations of a 'green' and social culture would be laid down, producing an ecology-based conviviality.

Among the severest obstacles will be those sections of the media that depend on large sales and therefore tend to pander to the public and to institutions promoting partial, short-term interests: business and trades unions, consumer organisations, etc. – not to mention commercial advertising. A real democracy means more than mere freedom of speech: that speech must also be able to be heard. This means that power over information resources must be equitably distributed. The present situation, however, is that the dissemination of information is governed by money, so that the richest can shout loudest and influence citizens the most.

Public education would greatly benefit if the media were also to adapt their other programmes and articles. At present, most entertainment favours a wasteful lifestyle.

In view of the drastic change needed, many activities of today's environmental movement appear trivial and, worse, become obstacles to the requisite growth in awareness. Endeavours towards more public transport, recycling, less harmful packaging materials, more municipal greenery, filters in factories, etc. – however valuable in themselves – obscure the necessity of freeing ourselves from destructive 'productivism' in its entirety. From the ecological point of

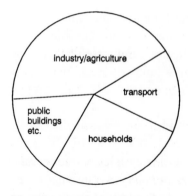

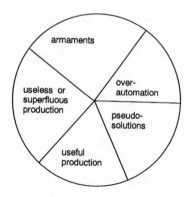

Use of energy in a rich country

The usual way of presentating data, for instance on energy consumption.

Another form of presentation may throw a clearer light on what we are actually doing.

view alone, there is, as already pointed out, no longer time nor space left for the cleaner production and recycling of unnecessary goods.

Moreover, the general focus by environmental groups on people as consumers not only reinforces the idea that production follows our needs and wishes, but also keeps people in the straitjacket of a sub-role. We are not only consumers but also inhabitants, workers, managers, parents, citizens. Too much stress on consumption patterns may obscure the necessity of making people politically aware, and mobilising them to become 'producers' of a new society themselves.

Hence the need for information and education being oriented to 'dark-green' ecological awareness and to fresh thinking about economics and society. Moreover, the information should try to be as 'answerable', as two-way-organised, as possible. (37)

To conclude with H.G. Wells: "Human history becomes more and more a race between education and catastrophe." (1920!)

FLEXIBILISATION

Our economies must be stabilised and made more self-reliant and self-sufficient again. (38) To achieve this would require, above all, the *liberation of our economies from the compulsion to growth* which the present money system generates.

What would this mean for Capital and Labour – during the change and for keeps?

It would require a different, *more flexible way of remunerating capital* (assuming that the role that capital currently plays in our societies and its relation to 'labour' will not yet be changed more drastically). A decline in the income of a business may be normal or temporary (less demand, shortage of raw materials, etc.) and will mean less income for the capital invested in that business. This should not, however, automatically result in the withdrawal of investments, thus putting an end to the business altogether. (Not automatically at any rate: there may be other reasons to stop it.)

The disastrousness of the present system can already best be seen in its effect on the peoples working most closely to nature's limits. Farmers and fishermen, who have had to invest in expensive modern equipment, are often in the position of having to pay their banks fixed annual sums, whereas yields from the soil and the sea fluctuate, with temporary fallowing even being necessary and natural.

The same – running up against natural limits or fluctuations – will sooner or later hold for other businesses as well.

The flexible remuneration of capital should not only be applied in relation to natural limits or fluctuations in demand, but also according to the usefulness of the type of production from the ecological and social point of view. Constructing windmills or running a crèche, for instance, would thus be supported with cheap money, whereas for the production of more luxurious goods or services only dearer money would be available. (One could think of a kind of 'eco-taxed' interest.)

With regard to labour, such a change would also require *employment to be organised more flexibly*. In my opinion, it should no longer be linked to the production of a single product or service, nor tied mainly to production for the market.

For example, if a shoe factory has met normal demand in its region

(with good, repairable shoes), the machines could slow down to meet
only supplementary demand, and the bulk of the workers could then
move on to other work in the region. (There is enough work if we
look further than mere production of commodities.) Factories operating continuously and at full capacity is really primitive, based – as I
suggested already – on cattle and bread: an *agrarian atavism*!

The result would be a variation in work, which happens to be the
desire of many workers! It would, moreover, further their development. And what about intellectuals regularly doing some manual
work, and manual routine workers being regularly engaged in quite
different work? (39)

One of the first steps would be to shift taxation (VAT, unemployment insurance
etc.) from manpower to energy, thus slowing down automation and the use of energy, machines and chemicals, and promoting labour-intensive methods and services.

The usual argument for continuous operation of a factory or other business is that it is a waste if machines do not work at full capacity. But this again is a view rooted in a partial interest – i.e. as seen at the level of the business – and not from a wider point of view: society, environment, the future – the overall interest. From the latter viewpoint, constant output from the machines can become harmful. Whether we are concerned with regionalised or wider production, the criterion should be: do we need the product? And: does the (global) ecosystem allow its production? If so, how many? what quality? can it be repaired? re-used? etc.

As for employment, one reason for maintaining some unemployment, it is said, is to keep the price of labour at a reasonable level. Similarly, the present system needs rich people in order to keep money available for saving and for investments. It is clear that both these situations may no longer be necessary in a more humane and intelligent economy.

Finally, labour should not continue to be taxed as is now the case in many countries. At present, there is a premium on using machines and fuels, and a tax on using human power. This should be reversed, as a matter of urgency.

HOW MUCH MARKET?

Within ecological and social limits (including, of course, the interests of the Third World), one could maintain a *self-restricting market economy*, balancing private initiative with collective needs. (40)

Our democratic systems should widen their scope to encompass fully the economic field, i.e. citizens should have more say in the production of goods and services. Major investments should be brought under (more) democratic control.

Is this going a bit too far? Even today, it should be remembered, commercial investments are often subject to certain permits and other boundary conditions, for example with respect to siting, nuisance, etc. Moreover, in businesses in modern countries, investments are discussed in the works council. (I do not plead for entirely new structures and measures, only for proceeding more firmly in the direction which history (= we) is already following!)

Such economic democracy – as the logical extension of present-day political democracy – should of course have its basis in the whole society. All citizens, both free and responsible – that is with a developed sense of ecology and the world community – should transcend their partial interest and keep their activities within the limits set by our ecosystem Earth. (41)

Within strict boundaries and regulations, competition could well be maintained, rather as is the case within animal herds: restricted and constructive, not destructive. *Competition does not require growth*. It can operate and function very well within an overall stable, 'zero-growth' system.

The more we have a 'steady-state' economy (cfm. Herman Daly), the more freedom we can allow the market, the fewer regulations we will need! As Daly (1980) puts it: "In all cases the guiding design principle for social institutions is to provide the necessary control with a minimum sacrifice of personal freedom, to provide macrostability while allowing for microvariability, to combine the macrostatic with the microdynamic."

Moreover, *growth does not equal development*. Daly again: "Growth is an aberration, not the norm. Development can continue without growth and is, in fact, more likely under a steady-state economy than under a growth economy."

Daly envisages a combination of three institutions:
- for distribution (with a minimum and maximum limit on income and a maximum limit on wealth);
- for birth control (by means of transferable birth licences);
- for controlling the use of resources (by means of depletion quotas). (42)

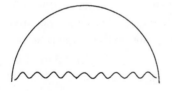

Economic variability within overall (ecological) boundaries (cfm. Herman Daly).

Daly thus reconciles efficiency and equity. In his words: "The market is not allowed to set its own boundaries, but it is free within those boundaries. Setting boundaries is necessary. No one has ever claimed that market equilibria would automatically coincide with ecological equilibria or with a reasonably just distribution of wealth and income. Nor has anyone ever claimed that market equilibria would attain demographic balance."

TOTALITARIAN?

The crazy and catastrophic freedom which large groups in the First World have won does not tolerate even the mildest restriction, because of the compulsion to growth. The privileged majority (those fully profiting, plus all those who are well-paid and dependent) and their media — most media — are now hurrying to label ecologists and the green movement 'totalitarian'. *Yet it is this very 'over-freedom' which makes the measures required for survival appear to be nasty, totalitarian limitations.*

Those people term as 'totalitarian' whatever impedes them. They do not realise that, firstly, their own positions and activities are ruled by a totalitarian compulsion to growth, the very catastrophically compelling situation that begs urgent alteration and, secondly, that their freedom has very commanding and restricting, in short totalitarian, effects on others. Not least on our grandchildren... ('Laisser faire, laisser détruire'). (43)

LIBERATION

It is not only the alienation of the labourers that would be overcome (they would no longer, through their work, be increasing the factor ruling them), but also that of the owner. There is hardly an owner or manager who enjoys paying too little for labour, energy, materials or natural resources. No entrepreneur or manager likes to pollute and destroy the environment. Today, however, he or she is often forced to do so.

Thus, the new economy would also, and foremost, mean *liberation for the business owner or manager*, at last enabling her/him *to slow down at any moment, to be careful, to alter or even to stop* (yet without bankruptcy, without immediately losing the place obtained in the market, and without upsetting employment or the income of the personnel, etc.). This means liberation from the present domination, yes tyranny, of finance.

This liberation would also mean that more people gain access to the market. The financial barrier which at present forms an obstacle for many entrepreneurs wishing to start a business would be much lower.

In short, what I am advocating is *freeing production, freeing enterprise* – not to be confused with traditional 'free enterprise'!

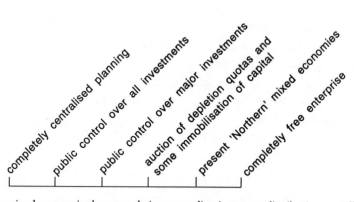

The mixed economies have regulations regarding income redistribution as well as for dangerous products, trustification, settling, pollution, import/export, etc.

All systems, except the completely free enterprise system, can have a scale of regulatory taxes, prohibitions, subventions, levies, restrictions, ecotaxing etc., ranging from heavy to light.

Moreover, variation is possible according to the geographical and administrative level: global, continental, sub-continental, multinational, national, regional, local. Global restrictions could be situated in the left part of the scale, permitting regional and local freedom more to the right.

EVEN MORE PLANNING?

Let's have a look at an everyday occurrence.

An entrepreneur who wants to start a business usually has to go to a bank for the necessary financial support (a loan). The bank will very probably help only those enterprises 'with good prospects', i.e. those that promise quick, high or certain returns. (44)

Why not organise things so that entrepreneurs who wish to start or innovate go, say, to an economic committee of the local council (hence democratically constituted) which has the money in trust and is authorised to decide on its use, taking into account wider interests than a bank could possibly do? (45)

I will pursue this peculiar line of thought and dare to suggest that it cannot any longer be left solely to the businesses themselves to decide on the use of their capital and profits.

First, let us not forget that, whether owned by a bank or by a business, all money comes from the joint effort of a nation or a region. Moreover, it has been taken away from other people or from other regions with a shortage (through the legal transfer of interest and dividend, or by making a profit on the consumers, or by paying too little to suppliers, etc.). And it has probably been paid for heavily by nature as well.

Secondly and above all, there are the ecological limits. If we do A, we do not do B and can perhaps never do B again.

Consumers may be overjoyed with their compact discs, to use our old example, but perhaps we simply cannot afford to produce them at all in view of the urgent need to restore photosynthesis, fight pollution, etc. or in view of the need to produce useful products or repair neglected social services. Perhaps we should have remained satisfied with LP's.

If so, decisions on what to do with the profits from LP's and record players should not be left to the producing companies, for they will reinvest in the development and marketing of CD's and CD players – quite logically from their point of view, and probably pleasing many music-lovers.

Such an approach towards investments which takes greater account of society as a whole and the environment: is it totalitarian? Or intelligent? Diverting money (and thus the opportunity to buy la-

Poster Aktie Strohalm

Save the world, so let's get rid of this jungle

bour, science, energy, materials, natural resources) from other purposes for the development of the CD (and soon the DA-tape) is in a
way also totalitarian. And so is obliging people to switch to the CD
because the LP is 'out' and shortly to be discontinued.

Revolutionary? Perhaps it is only when one fully realises the
imperative need to save the environment (remember: the basis of all
economy, of all production and of all life) that these suggestions for a
more planned and collective economy may appear less provocative.

It is, I recall, A or B. Producing better bread or making yet another
kind of music player. Planting trees or creating yet another car model.
Healthier, better educated children or faster trains and aeroplanes. Still
more household appliances or birth-control programmes. 'Rhinos or
rockets'.

Conventional wisdom is that profits mean that the production
which generates them meets an important or valid need or desire and
that that production should therefore continue. However, one could
equally well or better say at some point that a need or desire which
has been met (except of course for goods and services which are

needed continuously: consumables such as basic food, electricity, tapwater, public transport, etc.) has been satisfied and that the productive potential used for that purpose should be diverted to something else, to one of the next items on the priority list of society.

RESPONSIBLE BUSINESS

There is more. Freeing production from the whip of quick and high returns, from the financial world breathing down one's neck – because that's what's behind it all – could put an end to the way production at present attracts the get-rich-quick, the rogue producers and cowboy tradesmen, and could give (back) more chance to the serious, socially-minded businesspeople and to the many able craftsmen who would like to operate on their own or in a group of equal partners rather than being obliged to work as just an employee, as is so often the case now.

A socially-minded entrepreneur will accept this restriction of his/her freedom. In fact, she or he will positively welcome it! Haven't most of us brought children into this world? And won't there be enough for our entrepreneurs and their collaborators to do, once work has been organised in a much more varied way?

It may be that the change of control over investments advocated here could be brought about by ecotaxing, i.e. by making CD's and DA-tapes (say) simply too expensive and unattractive to produce. (I will return to this further on.) However, it is also essential that the attitude of the entrepreneur and his/her relation to society as a whole changes, that she or he does become part of the community, truly serving the public (as they often like to present themselves). If this attitude of restraint and social consideration is only to be brought about with reference to ecological and more remote ('godlike') criteria, it may actually impede a truer, more internalised change in humankind – a small step back towards a 'We'-culture, from an 'I'-culture gone way over the edge.

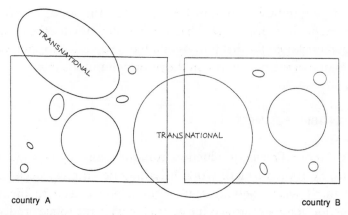

country A   country B

Continous scaling-up

This results in a few very large businesses which control the market (some transnationally) and a number of small ones that manage to operate in the margin.

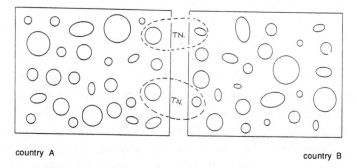

country A   country B

Decentralised economy

Production will be spread over many enterprises. Optimum efficiency (which includes environmental and social care) should be the criterion. One can still have differences in size and scale, as well as businesses that operate in several countries. As regards competition, in a stabilised, non-growth economy it can change back from being destructive to being corrective.

MOTIVATION

I realise that this argument for more planning, or at least more democratic control over investments, is at odds with even the restricted free market system, which I hope can nevertheless be maintained. This is precisely the kind of problem yet to be solved and worked out.

We now realise the dangers of both too much freedom and too much bureaucracy. On the basis of a better analysis of our economic system, the general desire for more equity among people, a better ecological awareness and our whole culture probably returning or evolving to increased conviviality, we will surely find a more stable and intelligent system which satisfies most people.

It should be recalled here that there is enormous scope in the extent to which an economy can be planned – remember Daly's idea of limiting only energy and materials – and that planning should not be associated with a one-party system. Nor does stabilising the economy mean that there would be no scope left for competition and micro-dynamism (compare a herd of animals).

Humans   **Animals**

How natural is our modern variety of competition?
If a herd of antilopes turned competition into a system, it would soon become blind to such dangers as ecological destruction (the lion).

Would people like to join in this operation? What motivation do people have to work, to serve, to produce (well)? In our present system, there are not many workers whose prime motive is pleasure in their job; for most, it is mainly the salary and the earned ability to buy goods. There are certainly a number of entrepreneurs who take pride in supplying a good product, but for the majority of present-day businesspeople, the main motives seem to be profits and perhaps status and freedom.

Should our new society, with its new economy, be based on altruism and on idealism? Surely, competition and discrimination are natural or have become so? Hasn't egoism become more 'natural' than altruism? On the other hand, are ants, which know that their own interests rely on acting collectively, then idiots? Or Pygmies, Papuans or Amazonian Indians? Or communities like the Amish and thousands of villages and small urban districts all over the world where community sense still exists and forms the *sine qua non* of survival?

If only our self-interest could be extended so as to encompass our grandchildren's children and their environment... Or would even this effort be too unselfish for us?

As mentioned, attitudes do change in cases of emergency like the outbreak of a war, a flood or an earthquake. Solidarity can suddenly emerge (as well as hostility...). There may be a future in creating medium-sized units for working, living and leisure, in which the individual feels at home and is protected and appreciated – somewhere he or she belongs. It would be rather like the old family or the village or the urban street, like the workshop or the old factory.

An overall cultural change, in which present-day over-individualisation is diminished, is of prime importance in this respect. It is only at a higher level that the individual can evolve and transcend, to some extent, her or his present isolation, which is nowadays his or her logical protection against a rather cold society focused on achievement and competition.

This would be a step forward for civilisation. However, it may be wiser – in any case where populations are firmly over-individualised and atomised – first to progress from self-interest (cfm. Daly). (46)

A serious obstacle to change is rather inherent in our democratic systems themselves, where politicians rely on large fractions of the

In some tropical regions, monkeys are caught by putting fruit in a jar with a narrow opening. The monkey grabs the fruit, then the hunter comes out of his hiding place and grabs the animal because it won't let go the fruit and therefore can't get its hand out of the jar. How much do modern humans differ from monkeys?

electorate whose partial, short-term interests (self-interests!) are consequently more encouraged than discouraged.

Another difficulty is the relative domination, in most professional bodies and institutions, of the larger companies and more powerful businessmen over the smaller ones. 'Mr. McDonald', for instance, speaks on behalf of the small snackbar keepers while at the same time his 'hamburger palaces' are pushing them out of the market. The rich farmers who are able to attend meetings dominate the farmer associations, to the detriment of the interests of the more numerous smaller farmers. (By the way, the difference between big companies and normal-sized ones, between remotely and directly or self-controlled companies could play an important role in the coming process of change.)

Probably the best approach for now is one of *balance*. We need a system that allows two sides to stay in balance: freedom and commitment; work and leisure; the individual and the collective/the community; self-interest and public interest; personal activities and social activities. A true balance, both at the individual level and at the level of society.

As many people have pointed out, in many, mainly North-European countries (47) the capitalist system has already undergone substantial social correction; it is a matter of firmly pursuing this road, for the sake of traditional justice and modern eco-care. (48)

1953: 207 bilj. K.cal.

Poster Aktie Strohalm   1976: 653 bilj. K.cal.

Basing himself on authentic facts, the Swiss artist Jörg Müller has pictured the transformation of a city centre in a rich European country over nearly 25 years. You or your parents will have experienced the similar 'modernisation' of an urban or rural environment. We calculated the increase in energy consumption during that peri-

The distinctions between our roles should diminish. More employees should, perhaps partly, become entrepreneurs, and owners
should also do some work as employees (or rather as members of
groups which perform certain public tasks and essential production).
The gap between capital and labour should be narrowed, as should
the gap between production (producers) and consumption (consumers), and between recreation and creation/production.

Let's hope that in a new culture, the gap between the individual
and the collective will have shrunk and that we function more like
members of a large family or a tribe. It is the larger group (tribe,
region, nation) that in most cases helps to shape the culture and the
collective norms and consciousness, the joint morality, the 'higher
self'. (Sure, mobs following a bad leader can go the other way. In that
case it is, conversely, people's individuality that must oppose the mass
trend.)

To sum up, the more sensitive we are to society, the less we need
control from others, from the collective, and the more individual
freedom we can be allowed and can enjoy! As for the economy, the
more we respect the overall restrictions, the more freely we can
operate. The greater our awareness of our material, physical interdependency and, hence, togetherness, the stronger the basis for real and
worldwide cooperation, for human conviviality.

To conclude this section about motivation with an important correction: changes come about because there is a *material* need for them,
not because people get new ideas. People become susceptible to
change because they can't manage the way they did. And because
there is the prospect of workable change. Therefore, the main source

---

od: *it was more than three times greater!* Conclusion: if we manage to reduce our energy consumption by two-thirds, we will return not to the 19th century, but to a
wealthy, quiet and enjoyable society. What's more, nowadays we can make much
more efficient use of energy than 25 years ago, so we will be back in the mid-sixties, say, when the Borderlands were singing: "I've got a job, a room, a bike and
I've got you. What do we want more from life, ain't it true?"
For a country like Holland, it is: Forward to the mid-sixties!

of motivation is emerging from smog and from tapwater becoming polluted, from farmers going bankrupt and the like! And conversely from the possibility of clean and stable production, of tasty products from organic farming, of experiencing the friendliness of the bicycle, etc.

The imminent eco-catastrophe can lead us to shoot at one other (as was reported during the 1972 oil shortage at a petrol station in the USA; also consider the potential for wars between nations or regions over water and energy resources...). Alternatively, it can forge us together because of the need to produce 'neg-entropy': pass on energy, share tools, repair goods and help each other to get the carrots to grow properly. (To those in the rich countries who are now shaking their heads in pity, let me recollect that the image evoked here is not very different from the social and economic setting of the majority of the other peoples of our world...)

PRODUCTION BY EVERYONE

The new, stable and quiet economy, which must gradually displace the old rampant one, will not only be helped by the existing alternative solutions, but can and should, as said before, also be based on the many people, skills and structures that are currently unused: the unemployed, the craftsmen and entrepreneurs in difficulty, women, and those many people declared too old or too young, too slow or too inexperienced.

To my mind, everyone should work productively, that is labour for society, at least part-time. This means that society – that's us – has to create a sufficient number of jobs. There's plenty of work! It's just a matter of organising employment differently and adapting the system of social benefits.

The idea of the state paying everyone a guaranteed 'basic income', regardless of whether they have a job or not, is spreading. This would make it much easier to employ people (or rather: allow them to participate). To my mind, a basic income for everyone should be linked to a package of basic tasks. Everyone should contribute to the productive work needed in their own country or region. (49)

If we are going to close many of the existing factories and businesses or make them work slower, masses of people will become unemployed. A catastrophe?

Well, instead we could consider 20 hours a week for productive work, a proportion of the remaining hours being used for social work (i.e. public tasks, which may include helping to harvest crops or recycle waste) and the third part for our own work, hobbies and leisure.

Moreover, many processes now being done by fuel-consuming machines and by chemicals can be replaced by human labour, thus saving energy and the environment. Old crafts will be revived ('old'? Mankind had only just started them!), enabling people to restore their relationship with materials and to express themselves in a more creative way than in today's conveyor-belt work. (NB. The whole gap between modern work and leisure and between productive and social work is, I believe, part of the general decay and alienation in our societies.)

"My brother's unemployed... He fills his time with action groups, language classes for ethnic minorities, clubwork, neighbourly help and so on..."

Ill. Arend van Dam

A considerable reduction of energy consumption would allow us to further mechanise and automate the dangerous, dull or dirty work still needed.

A large labour force will be needed in organic farming, which remains the basis of all our activities and has allowed humankind to exist for thousands of years. Its prominence has now been taken over by the industrial sector, producing chemicals, cars, electronics, etc. – a fatal error.

Especially in the areas around cities, horticulture, fish and goat farms, etc. could be developed by the city-dwellers (individually or collectively, by a town quarter). At the same time, they would dispose of their organic waste on these same lands, thus shortening circuits.

In general, the lines between production and consumption would be shortened, and the gap between producer and consumer diminished, for instance by creating consumer councils.

Distribution would function at a slower rate – that is, less fast than now – and with more care and efficiency (fewer empty trucks on the roads, more transport by ship and rail etc.) Time must therefore be reserved for travel and transport, mainly by public means and in combination with cycling, for instance. The use of private cars will be restricted... One could imagine the use of permits according to certain criteria, or petrol rationing.

Much work, too, will need to be done in cleaning up the environment: rivers and lakes (and their beds), soil, old refuse dumps. And what about the restoration of hedges, bubbling brooks, orchards? And reforestation and combating erosion?

There is also great scope for jobs in the realm of repair and recycling. We will at last (or again) be able to give proper care to materials and goods – houses, iron, timber, textiles, vehicles.

The huge field of soft technology and renewable energy will also require a large labour force. Many garages in the motorised countries could convert to installation and maintenance of soft technologies: generation and conservation of energy, water, etc. And imagine the challenge of greening our cities and making towns and villages cosier and equipped with better facilities, so as to make people less inclined to leave or go elsewhere for fun.

Many people will be needed for disseminating information, for training and teaching. Much productive work should allow for simultaneous, incorporated education. We will at last be able to give our young people (who, by the way, should also be involved in some productive, 'real-adult' work) the attention they deserve. Adult classes will be necessary, to explain about ecology and economy, and to teach people how to work and how to participate and communicate. Needless to say, we should give more help to the old, who, for their own benefit, should also be engaged in work for as long as possible – work which we will at last be able to organise in a normal and unstressed way.

One of the reasons that laws and regulations do not work is the lack of control. So here again is an opportunity for many new jobs. It would, however, not be desirable to enlarge the traditional police force, except for fighting pure crime (including crimes against the environment). It would be preferable to have controllers who are educators and instructors in the first place, teaching people new techniques, methods and behaviour. In the long run, it would be ideal if every citizen became a bit of a (kind!) controller – I mean a concerned, co-operative, supporting member of the community.

ECOTAXING

Calculating prices by incorporating all the real costs so far left out or ignored (i.e. internalising external costs) and/or by ecotaxing (it's more or less the same, but the first may include more social costs) might prove an important instrument in changing the entire economic picture. For instance, the moment the price of energy reflects its damage to nature, employment, etc., *all economic programmes will have to be recalculated and consequently will be completely altered*. It will no longer be profitable to sell fresh Dutch flowers in Tokyo or in New York, to give just one of a million examples.

Such 'full-cost pricing' will not be an easy operation, to assign to energy, materials, goods and services their true ecological price (cfm. Roefie Hueting, Ernst von Weizsäcker, Umwelt und Prognose Institut, Heidelberg, and many others). Suppose it was introduced in one country. Businesses established there will immediately complain about unfair competition and will threaten to leave. To what extent will it disrupt production and distribution? Here again, the answer is:

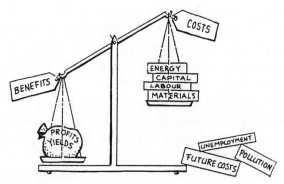

How we calculate now ...

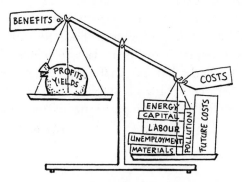

... and how we should start calculating as soon as possible.
If most of the costs now left out of consideration are properly internalised, without
being corrupted by short-term interests, economic analysis and planning will
change completely.

it ought to be done, so let's do it. Combined with taxing imported goods
according to their burden on the environment and resources (i.e.
taking into consideration what they are made of and how they are
produced, their use and whether they can be repaired and reused),
other countries will be strongly influenced to follow the example.
And let's not forget: in all countries environmentalists are pushing the
idea of ecotaxing and of internalising costs.

However, there are serious problems with ecotaxing. Ecological
and future costs are very difficult, if not impossible, to evaluate. And
how to prevent business and its scientists and politicians and other

mainstream experts (the great majority) calculating so as to continue business as usual, at best corrected slightly and therefore far from sufficiently? Would it not be more logical to simply start reducing or banning cars, high energy consumption, factory farms, CFC's, armaments, cadmium, one-way goods, etc.?

Ecotaxing could favour the richer enterprises and speed up the enlargement of scale (extension of enterprises, mergers, etc.), with the 'poorer' enterprises being pushed out even quicker. We might sell out nature, the environment and its resources to the highest bidders, to the richest buyers. (One of the first slogans of the Dutch environmental group Aktie Strohalm was: 'The polluter should not pay but should stop polluting.' 1970)

It is also true, however, that expensive fuel will encourage labour-intensive production and that ecotaxing will favour enterprises that are less mechanised and 'chemicalised'. Cadillacs etc., having become too dear, will disappear. Moreover, high taxes and penalties do indirectly compel enterprises to clean up and prevent pollution.

For some commodities, available for a happy few (flashy cars, yachts, etc.), it would be unwise to allow the continuation of produc-

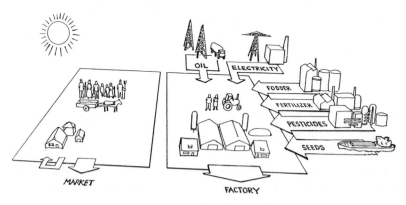

The vulnerability of modern enterprise, exemplified by an old and a modern farm. In supplies and sales no hitches can be tolerated. It is estimated that the net result of industrial agriculture is negative, if we had the intelligence and courage to take into consideration the environmental costs now known to us. Our grandchildren will know and experience many more!

tion, albeit 'eco-taxed' and considerably reduced, because this will keep more envy alive than is good for the general change to more conviviality. (Cfm. Daly and Cobb, who have devised tax policies that are pro-business and anti-accumulation of great private wealth.)

It will require a majority to support adequate ecotaxing before it can be introduced – and a majority in many countries. This means a heavy power struggle in our parliaments and in our societies as a whole. The green movement, possibly supported by the 'awakened' parts of the traditional social movement (socialist, Christian and humanist/liberal) and perhaps by parts of the small-business sector, has to face the entire 'no-nonsense' establishment which still controls production, employment and consumption. (But struggle it will be, as it always is to achieve change.)

Finally, let's not forget that the 'eco-socio' attitude should get into our marrow, our hearts and our heads. Would this happen if it were introduced through the purse?

Be that as it may, one could say that, in general, a strategy should be varied and pluralistic, capable of operating at various levels and in various sectors of society and the economy.

Conclusion: it would need further study to see whether and where ecotaxing will help or, on the contrary, block the U-turn to be carried out to the extent which our survival dictates. To my mind, a number of different approaches should be taken to achieve a proper U-turn – including less market-oriented ones. Ecotaxing may be one of the important ones, to be embedded in a larger and deeper Change.

LESS PUBLIC INCOME?

Surely, less production would mean less income for the state and consequently for collective needs? Thus, there will be less money for the economic infrastructure, for health care and education, for social allowances, development aid and for combating pollution.

Various points have already, at random, been made about this situation. The essence is: *in the new economy there will be far lower costs for the state.* The internalising of costs will mean that less costs are being passed on to the nation. Everyone will be more or less productive, including the young and the old. Pollution is likely to be reduced considerably. Production, and life in general, will provide more learning situations and will also be less stressful and unhealthy. People will no longer immediately take time off and rush to a doctor if they feel unwell. The stream of toxic and unnecessary wastes will be minimised. The Third World will no longer need our dubious charity. Armament will at last globally be on the retreat – another important economy measure for many nations. (The u.n. report 'Our Common Future' states: 'Nations must turn away from the destructive logic of an 'arms culture' and focus instead on their common future.')

We will have a much more de-stressed and stabilised and therefore durable economic infrastructure (roads, harbours, tapwater, power, etc.) which no longer needs constant modernisation and therefore high public expenditure.

Finally, the state, too, will be liberated from the compulsion to growth and from the strangling spiral of increasing loans.

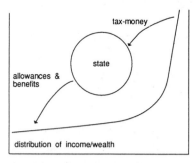

Much 'state' needed

The more costs are internalised ...

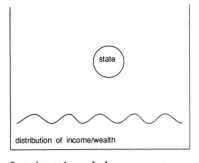

Less 'state' needed

... the less levies and subsidies are required

The same applies to environmental and social care. The more business and citizens look after themselves and each other, the less we need a correcting bogey-man.

BLUEPRINT FOR CONVIVAL

As early as 1972, a hopeful 'Blueprint for Survival' was drafted by U.K. environmentalists (Edward Goldsmith c.s., at the time described as pedlars of doom and gloom....). Today, there is a greater need for a similar programme of concerted action.

As I guess that change is only possible if the vast majority of our peoples engage themselves in it, the time now seems right for a *Blueprint for Convival*: ecology as if people mattered, to avoid a packet of draconian measures suddenly being dropped on people's heads. (I do not advocate 'eco-fascism': green colonels taking over and imposing environmental conservation by means of the whip. On the other hand, we must bear in mind that there is very little time left before we have definitely annihilated nature's regenerating capacity – that is, nature as we humans need it. I mean, we can't wait until everyone is ecologically aware.)

This programme of action should make it clear what has to be done at the various levels of our society and in the various sectors of our economy. It should define what should be done by the people: as consumers, as citizens, as employees or owners/businessmen, as rural or urban inhabitants, as parents/breadwinners or as members of an association, church, party or union. The same goes for organisations and institutions, for public authorities, government, industry, agriculture and trade.

The phasing of the actions in the various sectors of the economy and at the various levels of society – municipal, provincial, national, continental, global – is important. [Readers, get together, put your minds to it and sketch it out! The book 'Future Wealth' by James Robertson will be helpful, among others.]

The essence of the proposed 'Blueprint' is the conviction that partial changes are no longer sufficient and will sooner or later fail. Such changes should be part of a range of interlinked changes, together forming the Great U-Turn, the self-reinforcing Spiral of Progress.

The main thrust of such a programme has been sketched in this book: the operation of pruning back, the Big Shrink (that is, for the rich countries and the newly industrialised countries), while building

up another economy – self-reliant, normal-scale, stable, green, democratic, transparent, convivial. The Happy Shrink...

Not new

Although the analysis given here may throw new light on certain developments, the changes proposed in this book (and elsewhere in the green
literature) are not new at all. In fact, they have been developed or tried out by
mankind for millennia, centuries or decades: democracy, limits to wealth and
power, corrections of the free market, licences for investments and production, birth control, more equitable sharing, pollution taxes, photo-voltaic cells,
conviviality.
The ecological crisis, which is destroying the basis of our economies and our
very existence, simply compels us to accelerate these developments.

THIRD WORLD

In this operation, the rich countries (which must include Japan!)
should take the lead. We have no right to dictate to developing
countries what they should do; we should only show them that we
ourselves are changing course. On the contrary, when it comes to the
U-turn we can probably learn more from the so-called underdeveloped countries than vice-versa! (When will the 'rich' countries at
last recognise that they themselves are highly *un*developed?!)

It would probably be a good idea to help the Third World in the
same way as Europe was helped after World War II, by means of a
kind of Marshall Aid, in other words with gifts, not with loans. On
the other hand, this may result in the Third World countries continuing to buy our short-sighted technology and it may mean a continuation of the annexation of these countries into the global financial
circuit and market, dominated by the North. (50)

Be that as it may, like the rich countries, these countries also need
equipment for conserving and saving the environment: their soils,
their waters, etc. However, the most relevant solutions often have less

Northern help ...

to do with technical fixes than with getting organic farming, tree plantations (of the right kind!) etc. organised – similarly to the situation in the rich countries in fact...

The situation may be helped by getting things going in a number of countries at the same time. Perhaps it is possible to form clusters of countries or regions that can support one another during the transition phase (by means of trade, so as gradually to achieve a certain degree of self-sufficiency, by building up a shared, alternative money system, etc. See also Note 38.).

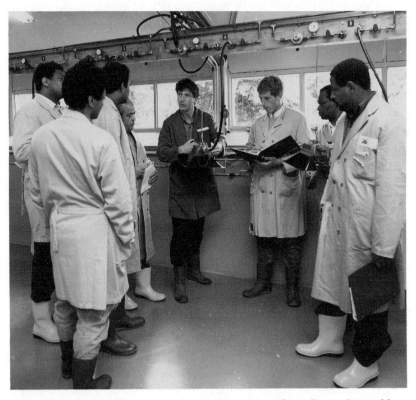

Industrialised Dutch agriculture attracts admiring visitors from all over the world. But perhaps old-fashioned farmers have more to teach them. After all, they managed for several thousand years... In general, the First World could learn much from the Third.

To tame or correct the multinational corporations would have to involve a specific operation. Trades unions (the forward-looking ones), consumers, 'de-hooked' shareholders, governments and environmentalists could perhaps find themselves in a concerted action.

As for the financial world, led by the powerful banks, perhaps we can liberate ourselves through better regulation of financial trade and investments. Or by introducing autonomous money, controlled by the community or society and directly based on the 'real economy'. (One of the many points which need further elaboration.)

With regard to overpopulation, which today is often dramatic, fighting poverty appears to be one of the main, though slow, weapons. But not with TVsets powered by hydro-electric dams. Nor with FAO-style Green Revolutions, which still ignore basic natural laws and restraints as well as the ecological wisdom of many tribes and communities. What they need – just as the 'wealthy' countries – is a real (dark) green revolution.

REGREENING THE PLANET

As for our main source of wealth – photosynthesis – it might be a good idea to use all the money available (not by means of loans!) for both an immensely important and an immensely inspiring undertaking which could generate worldwide solidarity and give the whole nasty operation of shrinking production a positive perspective: the *regreening of our planet*.

By doing so, we could:
- safeguard what soil is left,
- make new soil,
- fight famine,
- spread authentic wealth
- and, on top of it, absorb excess carbon dioxide.

This restoring of photosynthesis would seem to be the only justifiable use of the vast revenues we are now pulling in from the photosynthesis of millions of years ago. We ought to spend our petro-pounds, oil-dollars, coal-marks and gas-guilders mainly on replanting the world.

We ought to take an example from Richard St. Barbe Baker, whose 'Men of the Trees' planted over 26 trillion trees worldwide.

As we all know, the military is the largest item of expenditure on the world's budget. At the same time, the lands that nations so dearly want to defend (or attack) are being polluted, poisoned and eroded (partly as a result of the same military endeavours). If only we could harnass all the manpower, science, energy and materials now being consumed by armaments and armies, and divert it to combating erosion and desertification! (51)

THE LOCAL LEVEL

At the national, regional and local level, interlinked operations should be carried out everywhere, in order to convert our economies to true sustainability (organic farming, soft technology and tool-sharing, decentralisation, full employment, revitalising villages and dormitory towns and districts, etc.). To my mind, the main thrust of this will be at the *municipal level*, through activity undertaken by and within local communities. These are now burdened with the 'waste' of our societies and with the shortcomings of central governments which have been too lenient. They are coping with mountains of refuse, too many cars, etc. and also with unemployment, boredom, vandalism and crime. (52)

Support again from the U.N. report 'Our Common Future': 'The law alone cannot enforce the common interest. It principally needs community knowledge and support, which entails greater public participation in the decisions that affect the environment. This is best secured by decentralising the management of resources upon which local communities depend, and giving these communities an effective say over the use of these resources. It will also require promoting citizens' initiatives, empowering people's organisations, and strengthening local democracy.'

It should be stressed here that it is the government and more local public authorities that are most suited to helping finance the establishment of the facilities and structures by which people can start working on the new lines and consequently expand those facilities and structures. Examples include buying land from an old farmer for labour-intensive, organic horticulture, providing a building for a recycling centre, training people in energy-saving systems or financing the construction of fish farms, etc. (Remember that, at present, most governments support ordinary, 'modern' industry and agriculture with huge sums of money – money that could be used for much more intelligent purposes...)

THE NEW ECONOMY

Moreover, parts of the existing *shadow economy* (the do-it-ourselves economy; the now marginal, off-market activities in and around the home, among friends and in the community) will come out of the dark and prove their worth as building blocks for the new, convivial economy.

Existing alternatives could also link up and cooperate to form a kind of supportive network, however weak and incomplete, providing new momentum on which to build further. *If we brought together all the alternatives that have been realised throughout the world in various social and economic sectors, we would already have a complete utopia!*

The new, sound, sustainable production sector should not become a keep-the-marginals-and-the-poor-busy playground upon which the traditional sector looks down. From the outset it should be brought home to the public that growing healthy food, for instance, is far more important than making most of the goods now filling the shops; that it is as important to know where to buy something as it is to know what to do with it once it has been used; that a waste collector is as important as someone who produces something; that blue collars may be more vital for survival than white collars. And so on.

So the main features of this new economy are: low wastage of energy and materials; normally sized, needs-oriented production and distribution systems; regionally organised, transparent, democratic structures; organic-farming-based; as self-sufficient as possible (which does not exclude the possibility that, for the time being at least, Europe, for instance, may need hydrogen from the Sahara as a substitute for fossil fuels, and the Sahara in turn may need assistance in regreening).

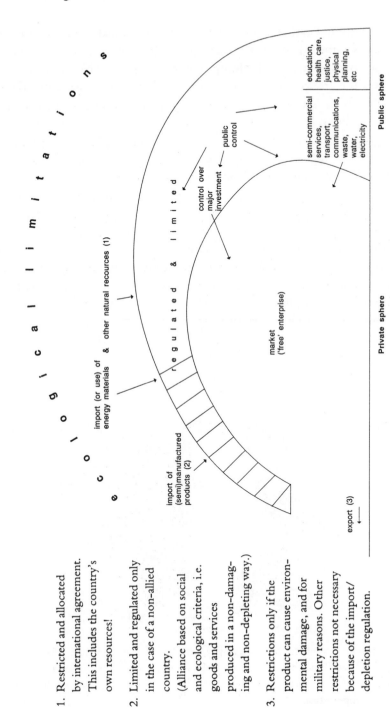

ecological limitations

import (or use) of energy materials & other natural recources (1)

import of (semi)manufactured products (2)

regulated & limited

control over major investment

public control

export (3)

market ('free' enterprise)

semi-commercial services, transport, communications, waste, water, electricity

education, health care, justice, physical planning, etc

Private sphere

Public sphere

1. Restricted and allocated by international agreement. This includes the country's own resources!

2. Limited and regulated only in the case of a non-allied country. (Alliance based on social and ecological criteria, i.e. goods and services produced in a non-damaging and non-depleting way.)

3. Restrictions only if the product can cause environmental damage, and for military reasons. Other restrictions not necessary because of the import/depletion regulation.

Festivities rather than moto-crosses; fine meals and community parties rather than all of us going to Mediterranean beaches every year; participation in building our society rather than an obsession with the motor car. In short: qualitative, cultural 'growth', while developing technology in a more intelligent way, taking into account the limits and complexity of our biosphere and the law of entropy.

As for trade, it should be reduced to natural surpluses, i.e. the extras that each region or country can sustainably produce (because of specific soils, resources, climates, skills or traditions).

It will be important to come to grips with such media as television and glossy magazines, which go on promoting a suicidal lifestyle and keep the public hooked on goods, career and status (not only in the advertisments but also, more hidden and subversive, in the ordinary programmes and stories). The financial investors and their allies will immediately defend their interests by an appeal about Freedom of the Press (*their* press, *their* talking!) or by pointing out that the viewer can switch off his or her television set.

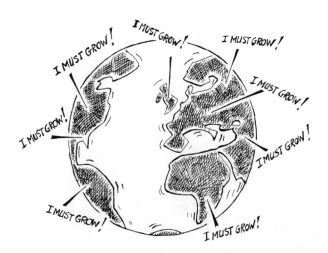

All countries want to grow, earn and export. But the Earth is limited. Moreover, a positive trade balance (more exports than imports, in money terms) in one country necessarily means that one or more other countries have a negative trade balance (more imports than exports).

INTERNATIONALLY

If international cooperative bodies like the European Community do not embark on this road, if we cannot 'convert' the EC, GATT, OECD, World Bank and FAO, we should turn our backs on them and try to go our own way. At present, 'Brussels' means further compliance with, and yielding to, the growth imperative; it means continuing to pave the way on behalf of expanding capital, which insists on ever more intensification, scaling up and so on. The question is: do we want a 'Europe of the multinationals' or a 'Europe of the regions' (cfm. De Rougemont and many others)?

TO SUM UP

We should:
- Prepare for a two-track strategy, breaking down the harmful large-scale and building up the green normal-scale.
- Regionalise.
- Make labour cheaper and energy dearer.
- Make the remuneration of capital and the organisation of labour more flexible.
- Fully internalise external costs and develop effective ecotaxing.
- Develop substitutes for imports.
- Liberate the poor countries from their indebtedness to the rich.
- Form alliances with other U-turning countries or regions, for supplementary trade and so as jointly to influence the wider world scene.
- Inform and educate – before, during and after.

The right balance between individual, free enterprise and collective intervention and planning is, I find, a difficult one. Some people think ecotaxing will bring about the necessary restrictions and general swap. I hope it will.

The main task – which will boil down to a power struggle – will be to weaken or annihilate the power of the present capital accumulations and bring investments under more democratic control (provided the democracy is ecology- and community-oriented). State-controlled financing and planning of the economy should, however, be avoided. So new forms of government, control and ownership should be elaborated and practised, as well as a money system in which money functions as a means of exchange and as a regulator and indicator, but in which it can no longer turn into a means of private (individual or corporate or bureaucratic) power which may harm our collective and future interests.

After this analysis of our economic situation and hints for a better strategy Part Three includes suggestions about what individuals and groups could practically start doing and what, luckily, people all over the world are already doing with joy and perseverance.

Under the whip of money-making, modern production and trade have developed to such a damaging extent that the net result of our economies has grown negative. Solution: a calmed down, stabilised economy; investments under democratic control and production remaining within ecologically sound limits; and money (capital) no longer a master but a correcting and regulating servant: fodder for the horse and oil for the wheels.

Part Three

Part Three

Suggestions for Misconduct*

It may be useful to suggest what individuals or groups of people, institutions or businesses *in the industrialised countries* could do in order to contribute to the necessary Change and no longer be 'part of the problem'.

NB. For the necessary research and feasibility studies to be undertaken in the early nineties, see 'Future Wealth' by James Robertson. 'For the Common Good' by Daly and Cobb also contains vital suggestions on the subject.

INDIVIDUALS

I guess 'green consumerism' is on the rise almost everywhere. This is good but it is not enough. It should not block the road to still better remedial activities, such as consuming less, informing and encouraging other people and trying to change and reduce production, mobility, etc. in general. We now need consumers who are not only green but also politically conscious and active. (NB. 'Political' need not necessarily mean oriented towards party politics.) They may be active in an environmental pressure group, or, and often better, in a trade union, a business association or in a civic committee, a women's organisation or in a political party. Or in a sports club. (Yes, why not? At his local pub, a German university professor has started to try and

---

★   The word 'misconduct' was inspired by Shaw's saying and may seem strange in the eyes of the eco-activist who goes in for bulldozer-blocking and fence-climbing. She or he might find these suggestions very goody-goody; and too slow to save the environment.

change his town. Environmentalists should frequently leave their own circles and mix with other people.)

As for spreading information, bother thy partner, neighbour, colleague, the man or woman next to you in the train or the post office.

Needless to say, the households of green consumers are based on saving energy, water and materials, and on less (or no) car-driving, less meat-eating, etc. (Methods to support eco-wise consumers can be found in the Global Action Plan for the Earth.) (53)

At supermarkets and the like, pressure can best be brought about by a group of customers, rather than by an individual request to the manager.

Besides being consumers, we also live somewhere, a fact already hinted at. Here again, there are lots of things to undertake in order to make your town, suburb or village greener, safer and healthier. And more active and convivial.

Try to form a diverse group, preferably composed of some Friends-of-the-Earth-like people, a few progressive adherents of the dominant religion, one or two dehooking business(wo)men and a few alert oldies. (And one intellectual, dogmatic radical – no more.) Perhaps, to grab the imagination, start with a tree-planting day or a litter-clean-up day. (The only danger is that your newly-formed group will attract too many members who only think people should change their behaviour rather than those who realise the need for socio-economic change. Try to keep your group varied with regard to opinions. The best thing is to keep the valuable start-in-and-around-the-home doers in a supporters circle around the group.) This public activity can be repeated every year, ending up in some kind of festivity. (In Normandy, nature conservationists regularly work together with farmers in the countryside, and end with a fish, wine and dance party!) The group will meet with applause and acceptance. From this rather easy and humble start, one can gradually move on to the more difficult, the more 'structural'. There is plenty of literature available to tell you what other steps or activities can be undertaken to deal with waste, urban greening (don't forget edible green: fruit trees, raspberry bushes, walnut trees, etc.), major polluters, education and traffic. (Just to mention a few possible activities: distributing, in urban centres and nature sites, a polite leaflet to car drivers asking them whether it was absolutely necessary to come by car. Or helping your street or the streets to be turned into a residential precinct.)

To jump to the more difficult: try to put the authorities on the track towards making villages and suburbs more self-reliant. The more facilities we can reach easily – for work, care and recreation – the less we and our children need to look elsewhere. (A district in the Dutch city of Breda has turned some wasteland, where garages were planned, into a common vegetable garden and turned old garages into repair shops and other workshops. In many other cities of the world, similar activities are underway on a much more intensive scale, often because of poverty, like in the New York Bronx.)

This need not rely only on public financing. People can also contribute by giving money, by lending bits of land, by making buildings available, by giving their time or by making people on the dole join in to help perform useful tasks, etc. A centre for meetings and activities could be a school, a community hall, a recycling workshop or just a barn. And why not the town hall? (54)

As a voter, it is important – unless you are a downright non-voting anarchist who thus leaves power in the traditional hands... – to support green parties, which serve as indispensable signposts, or (dark) green representatives of other parties. The value of the green parties is such that you need not necessarily agree with all their points to support them.

As a parent, one could bring pressure to bear upon the school to give more attention to environmental and public matters and to promote relevant activities. (55)

The green consumer, who has savings, could well support the new environment-oriented funds. (But beware of the too clever ones now rapidly emerging in the traditional world of Finance!) One will receive less interest but one's money will be used in a better way. Ethical or social banking or investing, it is sometimes called. There are also schemes whereby people donate part of their monthly income to a 'good cause': peace-building, or Third World direct-aid projects, or environmental protection, for instance. At this early stage, it seems wiser to put your money into projects for consciousness raising and for informing people rather than in more technical projects like recycling centres, wind farms, etc. – unless these are again primarily

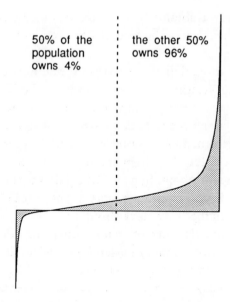

This graph, representing the division of financial wealth in Germany (the former western Federal Republic), shows why it is so difficult, in many countries, to change things. If half the population owns the major part of the wealth, they will not question the traditional (economic) path. Moreover, many of the other, less well-off half don't even vote any more.

Within the well-off half, most wealth is owned by only a small minority of very rich people, but this is not yet realised by the majority of the well-off's. (Graph by Helmut Creutz)

to attract and inform the public. Once we have a green tide, we will have plenty of means to build up the technical infrastructure. The best thing seems to be to try to invest in, or lend to, projects in your own neighbourhood (unless it is a rich one which should be helping the poorer districts).

Earlier I mentioned our task of informing and stirring up (gently, agreeably! Though sometimes losing your temper works even better...) colleagues in the office or factory where we work. I don't just mean getting used paper sorted separately. (Precious time is often lost in endlessly trying to get recycled paper and washable coffee cups (re)introduced. Please remain alert as to what are the main issues and what are side-issues. Let's avoid being paper-wise while production-foolish!). Nor is it even only about producing in a less polluting and

Think globally, act locally ...

Ill. Henk Groeneveld

"Look at all those busy people: greening their neighbourhood, reducing the speed limit in their street, supporting recycling ..."
"Excellent. Leaves our hands free for the major decisions!"

wasteful way – though these are often useful short-term targets. But I also mean informing people and starting discussions about the general insufficiency of technical means, the harmfulness of what is called 'progress'. And about the short yardsticks with which we calculate and our short-sighted idea of profit and efficiency. And about the need to reduce production volumes and the like. (In short, pass on this and similar books! See also Note 59)

'Light green' steps, reducing pollution etc. are all right *provided they are part of a wider 'dark green' strategy and consciousness-raising process*.

A final remark about general relations with public authorities. In those countries where social welfare has, quite rightly, been developed (either by social or human capitalism or by state socialism), people tend to rely heavily on the state, which may often impede the starting of things oneself. A small example: when they find too much litter in their street, caused mainly by the inhabitants, people are used to calling the refuse service. They could, however, organise a team to clean it up themselves, thus perhaps influencing their fellow inhabitants to become more careful. Also, many initiatives shipwreck because the public grant that had been applied for was refused, while other ways of procuring or raising money or of getting support from volunteers had not been sufficiently explored.

BUSINESS

NB. Many suggestions in this section also apply to the numerous institutes and offices, private or official, whose task is to support and serve the various sectors of the economy and of society by means of research and planning.

The essential approach has already been sketched above. Enterprises can't slow down or be closed down or converted immediately – and some should certainly usefully carry on for a long time! (Even a seemingly simple point like making the product repairable is usually in conflict with the enterprise's need to sell continuously and as much as possible.)

Some steps ranging from light to dark green: ecology courses for employees; encouraging commuters to use public transport or carpooling; internal 'environmental care' programmes; as for production processes: cleaner, and using less energy, water and materials; making the product easier to repair and/or recycle; influencing suppliers as regards their products (what they are made of and how they are made); similar pressure can be brought to bear on the business by banks when they are asked for a loan, or by accountants and assurance companies; studying the possibility of consumer participation; studying conversion possibilities; a deep-ecology happening for shareholders; a study to find ways of slowing down production. We can support general thinking about other ways of organising employment and capital remuneration. We may study closing down the business altogether (in a case where the product is harmful, unnecessary or, by structural U-turns in society, made redundant) and of creating other kinds of work in the region.

There is frequent discussion as to the best 'solution': plastic cups or cups which one has to wash up; plastic packaging or glass bottles (for milk and other drinks); recycling of the material in a product or re-use of the product; public transport or private cars; etc. Often, the ecological balance of both such 'solutions' is not very different, and business and environmentalists go on combating each other with ever new expert findings. The real solution, inspired by deep ecology and aiming at a really sustainable future, may well ask for a more radical change, for a more creative turn, and should be found beyond the limits of these short-run considerations. For instance the discussion about the one- (or more-) way bottle or plastic packaging or aluminium cans ought to be cut short by pointing to the absurdity of packaging a few gulps of a drink or of having a bottle first broken into pieces and then restored into a whole bottle again. We should remind people of the soundness of days gone by, when grandma poured out some syrup into a glass, which she then diluted with water and later went to the shop with an empty jug or bottle (cleaned by herself according to what had been in it) where it was filled with milk or wine or vinegar, etc. (as is still done in some very modern French supermarkets!). The same applies to the question of mobility and physical planning, or the question of energy supply and 'demand'. As explained, there is no time, money or resources left for costly pseudo or half-way solutions. The real solution (i.e. often a slowing down, or a conversion to quite different products, or even stopping all together) asks for some more courage and change, and lies beyond the limits within which present discussions usually take place. Most businesses can't help sufficiently; the overall framework in which they operate ought to be changed. Therefore, even the creation by companies of community panels with consumers and environmentalists in order to discuss environmental problems and policy (experiments in the USA) will not enable us to get away from half-way or pseudo solutions, and also involves a risk of being co-opted by business.

As an example in the world of finance, consider institutions like pension funds – usually considerable accumulations of capital and therefore important investors. They want to get as much and/or safe revenue as possible for the sake of their clients, who then have a correspondingly lower premium. They invest in the traditonal way and thus contribute to ongoing catastrophic developments (for instance urbanisation; such funds adore investing in real estate) which are making our society ever sicker and people ever quicker to retire. They would do well to develop a better analysis of the world in which they operate and of the effects of their functioning, and to start wondering whether they should not make choises for a future a bit further ahead and for general long-term interests instead of for specific short-term interests.

As regards the domination of the money-must-grow system over production and trade, barter systems can be of some help. The question however is: which activities should we, as a society, favour and which should slow down or stop? It is clear that useful activities must be supported; farmers and fishermen, for instance, should no longer have to work under unhealthy pressure from money-lenders. One possible alternative is eco-regulated interest. In some places, people have started their own means of exchange or trading-bond schemes. (In a way, the Keynesian remedy, but in a decentralised – local or regional – form, and, let's hope, as much 'eco-steered' as possible.)

With regard to the money system, I have already mentioned the difference between rich businesses (small or big) and businesses which have to work with considerable amounts of external capital (shares, loans) and which are thus, by producing, increasing the capital (and hence power) of funds, banks and rich individuals. This difference could play a role in a strategy of change, in the freeing of production and trade from money-making. (See also Note 59.)

In various business unions and associations, small owners or enterprises (rich or poor) could speak out against the dominant policies, which are usually defined by the large owners and enterprises and often unfavourable for the smaller ones. They should also start to raise general awareness with regard to the money-must-grow system. As regards state financial help for business (a wide range of schemes!), smaller enterprises could try, as a shorter-term target, to prevent such schemes continuing to favour large-scale enterprises.

Most employees, especially the lower paid, are glad to have a job and a salary. They go where their bread is buttered. They can and will help in producing in a less polluting and wasteful way, but will not be very susceptible to entirely new ideas. Perhaps one can find a more willing ear in higher ranks or with those who have more or less 'made

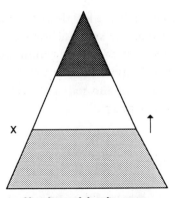

Number of businesses

In many branches of a growth economy, the situation is as pictured here. Because of continuous scaling-up and intensification, businesses (including shops, farmers etc.) are constantly pushed out, made bankrupt or merged into a larger set-up (bottom). At the top are the businesses that are likely to last for some time – few in number, but together representing a large proportion of production. Those in the middle all still think they will make it. However, the line marked x – the red line every business knows about – is constantly moving upwards...

and had it'. Some influential businesspeople become really dark-green and post-industrial – even though it is usually after their retirement. They can be instrumental in upsetting mainstream ideas, as a way of starting structural changes. I also have in mind people like Prince Charles of the u.k. and Queen Beatrix and her husband Prince Claus of the Netherlands, who have publicly voiced their worries about modern developments.

It is clear that businesses are usually caught up in a network of obligations and competition. One can't expect them to close or even to calm down. The necessary U-turn can only be brought about by a movement of society as a whole, surpassing the prevailing partial interests of each business or institution. The businesses and economic sectors that are harmful or unnecessary and should sooner or later close down or slow down – segments of the chemical industry, the arms industry, the motor-car sector, air traffic, factory farming, industrial fishery, agro-forestry, gadget producers – should not be the only ones to suffer. The burden should be borne by us all, by society as a whole. You can't always help the fact that you found a job in a nuclear power plant rather than in a solar cell factory, or that you liked fixing cars and started a garage, instead of fixing animals and becoming a vet.

This being so, each individual or group can decide whether to become part of the solution and start preparing for the U-turn, or remain an obstacle to real progress.

TRADES UNIONS

Most of what trades unions could contribute can be deduced from what has been put forward under 'business'. It is quite understandable that unions should strive for power and hence for a wide workforce membership and should therefore focus on the direct interests of that workforce – higher wages and so on. But it is an impasse, a knotting of your own hangman's rope. The result: greater dependence on capital and its – ever more automatic! – organisation of production. Moreover, consumption is increased. And the great ecological crash is brought nearer.

Many people have good expectations of worker ownership, ranging from enabling workers to buy or obtain shares in the company through to full, collective control by the personnel. The great danger under present circumstances, however, is that by doing so workers are made accomplices to a fundamentally wrong system which exploits

nature and the Third World. It is a further step towards total alienation. The only good aspect is that workers learn what management,
investing etc. mean.

The interesting set-up in the once run-down town of Mondragon
(Basque country), based on self-reliance, self-financing and workers'
control, no doubt has difficulty in achieving really environmentally-
benign production; and in not collapsing under the yoke of 'modern'
competition and the whole spiral of growth. (56) All over the world,
cooperative bodies have been set up by small entrepreneurs (e.g.
farmers) and have developed into ordinary businesses, which treat
their (former) owners as ordinary clients and may well even invest in
activities contrary to their interests.

All the same, trades unions could be instrumental in preparing for
the U-turn. Apart from reconsidering mainstream economics, they
could start rethinking their basic structure, which at present follows
the traditional pattern of production. Industrial workers, food &
agriculture, railway workers, the car industry – each has its own
(sub)union with its partial, often progress-impeding interests. The
confederation of unions should work out a new strategy, fit for the
21st century. Choices ought to be made and priorities fixed. Where
should work be reduced? Where developed? Where converted?
What can we unions still do usefully? Where are we still part of the
problem? Isn't small more beautiful? Should we be afraid of a development towards more small owners and businesses?

Should the system of paid work not be revised and the definitions
of 'work' and 'job' be enlarged? Should we not reduce the division of
the population into those with a job and those without? Should
members who are put on the dole (who's next?) not remain within
the union? What could be 'flexible employment' on our terms? Do
we discuss the idea of a basic income?

How can we improve democratic control over investments (an old
theme in the world of Labour!) without merely reinforcing the State
mechanism?

Start with training courses on ecology and non-traditional socio-
economics. Distribute books like 'Future Wealth' (and perhaps this
one) among the union's officials. (See also Note 59.)

In the Netherlands, the (two) confederations of trades unions take
part in a working party on environment and work set up by the major

environmental organisations. Among other things, this has prepared a joint report on the creation of new jobs in energy saving, pollution prevention and public transport. With the support of environmentalists, the refuse collecting services, which tried to resist privatisation of their sector, have developed a plan to turn them into sophisticated recycling services.

There are plenty of activities waiting to be invented which marry useful employment to environmental care. Incineration plants could be turned into regional recycling and re-use centres. Public transport employees could help to raise public awareness about the damage caused by the car system and organise public meetings to discuss a new transport policy. Future conversion of car service stations into stations to service environmentally benign technology has already been mentioned. There are enough preliminary and partial steps to be taken!

THE CORPORATE ELITE

I am afraid financiers, big shareholders, captains of industry and the rest of the corporate and financial elite form a particularly difficult lot to persuade of the necessity and the sanity of a U-turn. However, even in these circles new-age thinking, anthroposophic ideas and post-industrialism are penetrating. And don't some have 'green' children?

Most people still think the best things to leave their children are objects of value and money – money made by destroying nature and hence destroying the childrens very future... They should realise that the only way out of our crisis is through change. They would do well to invite 'greenies' and 'socios' to their Clubs, board meetings and training courses, and try to listen open-mindedly and -moodedly to their queer ideas.

These business and finance people are certainly in favour of eco-industrial projects – a new growth sector, isn't it? – and eager to collect money from citizens wishing to make green investments. Part of these activities will surely be helpful, which makes it all the more difficult for us to separate right from wrong. The main point is: *if you get sick after a meal in a restaurant, would you like to have the manager as your bedside doctor, or a more unbiased physician?*

An ideal strategy would be for them to help new, green executives and bodies to be efficient and to organise, while forgetting completely about quick profit-making, power-building, etc. And to give up their wealth and power and become normal, usefully engaged citizens. Since this is, however, hardly possible, it would seem wise to ask the rich and powerful – and all their servants and allies in the high places of government and official institutions – to retire quietly to their no doubt comfortable dwellings and leave society and business to a new green and social kind of people. (57)

As I said, I fear businesspeople will be very much against real change. (Light-green adaptations are okay.) Supported by the conservative and populistic mass media, they will ridicule every alternative attempt and wreck every truly U-turning activity. Perhaps even more difficult to cope with than with the old captains of industry and finance will be the layer below, the yuppies, the people of an often less wealthy background who now want to make it... How do we

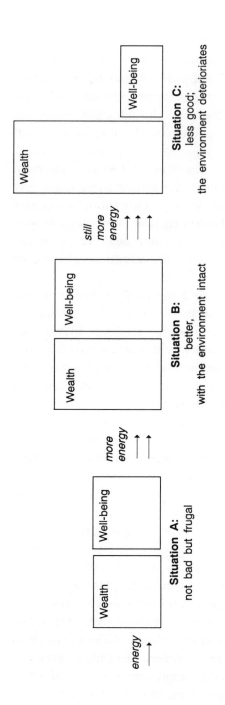

Situation A:
not bad but frugal

energy ↑

more energy ↑↑↑

Situation B:
better,
with the environment intact

still more energy ↑↑↑

Situation C:
less good;
the environment deterioriates

We don't need to go back to A!
A step back (forward) to B is enough

Human activity may be able to increase wealth and well-being, but a flip-over point can easily be reached beyond which the net result becomes negative, and general and future well-being seriously threatened. Reversing this process does not necessarily mean a return to the Dark Ages!

Precisely because of his knowledge and his consciousness (a gift from the Gods?), Man is capable of destroying his habitat, but also of restoring it. A pity that he has not yet embarked on a path that would at last distinguish him decisively from the other animals…

'heal' them? It's not easy even to get them to a doctor for a consultation! (58)

I should add that our present political and economic leaders, usually to be found on the right side of the political spectrum, should not be considered 'baddies'. (The left, which often has difficulty in thinking structurally, has done so frequently and have consequently always been amazed to find their own people, once in power, eventually behaving in the same way after some time.) Most of them truly believe in the traditional conception that furthering their business is the best thing for the economy as a whole, for the nation and for the world; that one needs rich people for their savings; etc. Just like you and me, they have been brought up with these ideas, which used to be pretty sound, but which have now become unsound (the virtues of the past which have become today's sins).

As mentioned above, a wholesome counterforce may emerge from the ranks of small- and middle-sized businesspeople and entrepreneurs who are becoming wary about being mangled in the wringer of Big Money. (59) Also, the wives and children of the – mainly male – VIP's may increasingly bother them with unwelcome eco-news and social ideas. Finally, of course, as organised or individual consumers we can bring pressure to bear upon the entire conventional structure of production, trade and financing.

Surely, some big-business people are honestly trying to do something to prevent the Earth's destruction? Haven't they and we all put a lot of children on this planet?

LOCAL AUTHORITIES

The importance of the local level has been stressed in this book. The steps which municipalities can start taking straightaway, and are luckily already starting, can be deduced from the above pages.

Local authorities can provide facilities for the re-use and recycling of 'waste'. Collecting waste from houses, shops, offices and factories is better than having it brought to containers, recycling centres, etc. (In Davis, California – see Note 33 – some 6 people are paid out of the revenues from collection of 4 or 5 separate waste fractions, part of which is sold to the recycling industry.) Municipalities and other local authorities can stimulate the prevention of waste; stop the use of hardwoods; stimulate the building of energy-saving houses; resist the money-pushed trend to build new buildings instead of adapting old ones; force demolishers to spend more time on the job and to separate materials for re-use. (All these have been put into practice in several Dutch towns, and surely elsewhere as well and better.) Municipalities should also try to reduce the intensity of commercial messages which currently take possession of our streets, walls, post offices and ears. It is another example of the 'tragedy of the commons'.

Municipalities must tame car traffic before it completely ruins towns, villages and the countryside. Beautiful cities like Prague, not yet 'demolishtorised', should now take the modern direction and opt for biking! Resisting high-speed trains (as has been done in the south of England, in Belgium and in the Provence) would be wise. Increasing the need for transport – an end-of-the-pipe approach – should be stopped and physical planning altered completely.

Try to build accommodation where people of different ages can mingle and be useful to each other (as in experiments in Sweden and elsewhere) and where there are cheap premises for starting small-scale entrepreneurs and crafts(wo)men.

Stimulate environmental education in schools, youth centres, adult education classes, etc. (but not as a fig-leaf for inadequate

MOON

EARTH

LOOK FOR THE SIX DIFFERENCES

environmental policies). Help citizen groups to run an – even small – info-shop in a busy street (sure, the expensive ground is worth it!) where they can give information to (and learn from!) consumers, housewives and househusbands, shopping farmers, tourists. (One usually finds nature- and children-oriented centres for environmental education on the outskirts of a town, and these are often just an extended children's zoo. They are not suitable for reaching the general public, only for demonstrating big machines like wind turbines and solar collectors.

I have dwelled long enough on the contents of environmental education in this book (e.g. Note 37), so I will not here devote a special paragraph to 'teachers'. Much is going on, from waste-free schools in Germany to curricula which include fieldwork on water and air pollution (Sweden, Britain, Netherlands). Apart from environmental education as such, it is vital that *all* educational disciplines and scientific research sectors freshly re-examine what they are doing, whether they are furthering sustainability or (blind) growth, i.e. real or pseudo-solutions, and how they too can convert so as to become part of the solution and no longer remain part of the problem.

Aiming at local self-reliance and self-sufficiency, and thinking of what people could start up comparatively easily and from their own liking to have good and cheap food, municipalities could stimulate organic horticulture, fisheries, goat farms, and the like. Activities involving repairs, re-use and recycling as well as alternative technology (more use of rainwater, windpower for a group of houses, combined heat and power generation, widescale composting, etc.) can also be made attractive.

It is important that such activities are developed in conjunction with local people, or that citizens themselves invent and develop them (within green guidelines!). But sometimes the town council should not hesitate, because time is running short, to take the initiative themselves. Here is a role for educators, as well as for community workers (see next section).

Town councils should therefore try to make available or lease land near the town, preferably within bicycling distance, where the jobless and others can grow and make useful products and do other useful things; where children and adults learn to care for animals and plants and learn useful skills. The organic waste from the town could be used on the land, thus closing again a natural circuit which until recently had done the job admirably for thousands of years. People would thus be encouraged to keep their waste as healthy (natural) as possible. The same would go for other rubbish, most of which can be repaired, re-used or recycled. (60)

It is not primarily a matter of money. Much can be achieved just by making different, creative decisions within the current legal framework and by demolishing fences between policy sectors, office windows and institutions. (Very hard work! One will find tough and unwilling 'nomenclatura' everywhere in the West too!)

It is important to raise the awareness of local people, their elected representatives and the officials. Showing films, for instance about 'eco-cities' and similar social and green alternatives achieved elsewhere in the world, proves quite stimulating. Like businesses, communities too should free themselves from the urge to grow, from prestige projects, from the traditional ways of attracting (capital-dictated) employment and income, from the obligation to stimulate commodity consumption and mobility.

Some of the New Work to be created has been sketched in Part Two of this book under 'Production by everyone'.

It is again clear that local communities can't just go along their own path of change alone. They can – and should – go some way, but sooner or later they will come up against barriers. Hence the importance of liaising with other public levels (provincial and national) in preparing for an overall change. For instance they need to get rid of the practice of stimulating growth by giving larger subsidies to the bigger municipalities and paying their officials more. They should also try to influence business – in a rather wider sense than just with a view to cleaner production processes.

Municipalities should really stand firmly together against central government, from time to time, in order to make it stop doing more of the things which 'choke' cities, villages and the countryside by stimulating practices which encourage waste, unemployed people, cars, pesticides, phosphates, etc.

Municipalities could contribute decisively to the forming of sound, ecofriendly, humane regions. In France, for instance, there is a powerful movement of rural mayors for revitalising the country ('Pour une France à villages humains').

This utopian sketch stands in stark contrast to the absurdity of the present situation, where numerous unemployed in the city fight boredom while a few miles away a handful of farmers labour away on vast expanses of land with the doubtful support of oil, chemical fertilisers, pesticides and proteins from faraway parts of the world. (NB. Old estates and parks should of course be spared!)

COMMUNITY WORKERS

It has been made clear that bringing forth a new, smaller-scaled, 'conserving and enabling' economy (as Robertson puts it) gives a major role to community workers, as well as to social workers, teachers, the active members of women's organisations and churches, etc. (And let's not forget the medical profession. Doctors and hospitals could do an enormous amount in furthering healthy food and wider eco-thinking and practice. It is a pity that they are not engaged much in preventive care and that they leave it to their social-medicine colleagues to bother about the more general (societal, environmental) causes of our illnesses.)

The training of community workers in the direction of a 'conserving and enabling' economy is therefore urgent. To their knowledge and skill should now be added dark-green ecology, a knowledge about the 'alternatives' all over the world and the enthusiasm to begin change in their area.

Admittedly, the apathy of most people, who are used to being passive, will hinder them, so it is important that the government and mass media support their efforts.

Public authorities should also help with money, schemes and other incentives to provide community workers with the necessary wherewithal, buildings, plots of land, etc.

One perhaps novel activity could be to put the inhabitants of a less privileged urban district in touch with organic (or converting) farmers in the neighbourhood, in order to exchange food for 'waste'. The inhabitants could buy healthy food for a reasonable price – possibly through an intermediary of a low-budget distributor or shopkeeper – with the delivering farmers going home with loads of good organic waste. I am aware that at present such a simple short-circuiting of producers and consumers would be confronted with strict regulations which, admittedly, often have a good reason for their existence, but which are also often too strict and restrictive.

Many other similar productive activities can be invented.

CENTRAL GOVERNMENT

As is the case with the lower levels of administration, the national government is divided into sectors: for justice, building, health, transport, economics, finance, etc. We now face such an environmental catastrophe that it is vital that the government creates a powerful taskforce of ministers and secretaries of state going crossways through the various departments. (It would be wise to do the same at the provincial and local levels.) Leaving the environment to one ministry is a failure because it can only try to clean up the mess the other ministries have made or have allowed businesses and people to make, or just try to prevent the worst excesses. Hence the need for an interdepartmental taskforce. If, however, here again mainstream financial and economic thinking dominates, it would be preferable to give more power to the Ministry of the Environment, provided it is not just light-green. How difficult it is to take a few fresh steps forwards!

Another important thing for central government and other authorities to keep in mind is that new ideas should be encouraged, even if these ideas are contrary to present government policy. A society which suffocates criticism of itself is doomed: think of the countries ruled by dictatorships or by one-party governments. Therefore, some public funds should go unconditionally to non-governmental organisations (NGO's) working for the new future. We must also remember that, in capitalist systems, the dissemination of information is a matter of money: the richest can cry out loudest. Somehow this has to be counterbalanced, because otherwise mainstream or pseudo-green thinking and the 'business-as-usual' ideology will keep on dominating people's opinions. To say nothing of mass market entertainment, which goes with the Bread: the opium for and of the masses!

Economically, the introduction of an eco-tax is important, together with the further 'internalisation' of costs which have so far been neglected or ignored. A whole constellation of measures must be taken to prepare for the U-turn and promote the first essential steps: stopping the favouring of bigger businesses and permanent scaling-up; bringing investments under greater control; stimulating import substitution and the general conversion of production; combating oligarchies and monopolies (except for some public services); taming or changing the money system; decentralising production; restoring agriculture to its prime place and quickly making it organic again; shifting VAT from labour to energy; and organising public debates and vast campaigns, jointly with the creative, green/social NGO's, to learn from the general public and to 'ecologise' and mobilise it in return. (In the Netherlands, the Ministry of the Environment discusses its campaigns with NGO's at an early stage.)

Governments should discuss joint activities with those nations that

have reached the same insights as themselves and persuade others that
have not done so yet. They should also try to change the policies of
international bodies like the World Bank, OECD, GATT, EC and FAO.

As for the short term, central goverments need only to look at the
programmes of green parties (in our great-grandchildren's history
books they will be called valuable pioneers!) to see where to begin;
like tightening up numerous emission standards, reducing car traffic
and production volumes (starting with vulnerable and harmful monocultures), preventing forest destruction, taming air traffic, organising
the return of used goods for re-use or recycling (from batteries to
cars), etc., etc.

They need to legislate such that doctors and environmentalists no
longer have to prove that a practice or a chemical is harmful, but that
companies have to prove the opposite before it can be marketed.

Universities should not be made too dependent on commercial
customers. These and other schools of higher education should, with
their students, carry out useful work for local authorities and the
public. More generally, they should re-orientate themselves towards
the building of a sustainable future instead of remaining addicted to
technical fixes and a science that only serves to continue blind economic growth.

As for the many preliminary studies which need to be undertaken,
see again Robertson's 'Future Wealth'. However, we do not have to
wait: many measures could and should be taken today. See also the
official Dutch report 'Concern for Tomorrow', which contains start-
ling figures and bold targets for reducing emissions.

Our parliaments and governments should fight our current, self-
destructive lifestyle by limiting advertising and converting it into
objective and eco-orientated consumer information. I am sure there
is a latent public majority to support this.

They should not be afraid of encouraging critical studies on the
present money system which, in my opinion, makes the wrong
feasible and the good too expensive.

In season and out of season, the ancient Roman statesman Cato
used to round off his speeches with the words: "By the way, it is my
opinion that Carthage must be destroyed." I dream of a modern
political leader or MP adopting the stopgap phrase: "By the way, it is
my opinion that production growth must be stopped."

Information and education are highly influenced and steered by the ruling powers.

A final word on the need to set examples. Ministers, officials and parliamentarians should, when possible, use public transport, walk or cycle. (This would, at the same time, give them a chance to meet ordinary people! Admittedly, this is not always pleasant if you often need to take unpopular measures.) In all public buildings, post offices, hospitals, libraries and the like, there should be various boxes for different types of waste. They should demonstrate that they are trying to save energy, materials and water. Make people get used to it. Make it normal.

THE MEDIA

A touchy subject. As said earlier, here again short-term financial considerations, if not plain private capital investments, favour or impose a populistic, non-educative content. And consumers become so comfortable with this that they want more of the same. Here again there is a self-reinforcing downward spiral.

Media owners and managers will of course deny that their broadcast programmes and newspapers are influenced or dominated by capital and business, and will fight every governmental interference on the grounds of Freedom of Speech and by pointing out that consumers ask for such programmes and articles. Or that people aren't forced to read their magazines or watch TV.

Populations that want to remain healthy and alert have to come to grips with this (unconscious!) 'drugs syndicate', to use another wild word. They should also resist the trend of 'infantilisation'. Readers who think I am exaggerating will probably be those who read only quality papers and only watch TV news and documentaries.)

There are possibilities for change through regulations and education, preluded by fresh public debate.

Journalists form an important bridge between facts and opinions, and the public. Though the medium – a newspaper, broadcast or magazine – for which they work has to operate in the present economic system, journalists have nevertheless (slightly) more room to manoeuvre than other employees, who have to pay close attention to ensure that the enterprise keeps on making a profit or that investors get their returns. Every journalist or television programme maker can pose the old question: am I part of the problem or part of the solution? How much am I caught up in the system? How conventional am I? Is my honoured objectivity in reality serving the old order? Do I explain to my public how things really are or do I play up to it, follow the line? Do I try to expand the frontiers of my task (set by superiors or the general office climate)?

I believe that serious and even disagreeable subjects can be handled and presented in an acceptable, yes inspiring and mobilising way. It is a matter for the programme-maker or journalist to know his/her job and to know what the public should do and is able to do. Most environmental programmes, for instance, end with a vague statement

The lifestyle and lack of awareness of the rich populations of the world are the real obstacle to survival.

that man is ruining the Earth and that he should stop doing so. At best, they ask us to become contributors to a conventional organisation for nature protection.

Television in particular makes people passive. But it is possible to change this by creating activities and facilities to establish a more two-way traffic. This would go much further than 'interactive television' which is still mediated and 'far-away' vision. For instance, one could have programmes linked with local centres, schools or NGO's where interested people (to be convened in the programmes themselves!) can meet afterwards to discuss the subject and eventually become active.

ORGANISATIONS IN GENERAL

Just a remark about the executives, leaders and active members (what the French call 'le cadre') in unions, organisations, associations and the like. If you can make them U-turn minded, you have won half the battle. However, they are often the very ones not so open to

change, as in my example of farmers' organisations, where the rich
members have time for the meetings and therefore dominate. Here
again: where do we begin? Do we try to change things from within
the organisation or should we organise something else? (Like some
groups of critical Dutch farmers who, rather than working within
their various associations, have set up a separate platform, retaining
both the option to support them again if and when they change their
policy sufficiently, and the option to make a definite break and start a
new association.)

It is also obvious that in associations, unions, political parties etc.
the more educated and articulate tend to dominate. Yet these may not
always be the best people to lead fresh opinion and it may even make
other more valuable people stay away.

The best, here again, seems a two-track strategy: trying to get the
'cadre' U-turn minded and trying to influence the members directly
(for instance, by handing out leaflets at their meetings).

ENVIRONMENTAL ORGANISATIONS

These should also increasingly prepare for the Great U-turn and gear
their regular activities to this change. Whether it is protecting birds,
fighting water pollution and nuclear plants or promoting green consumerism – every undertaking or campaign should be accompanied
by an effort to raise the awareness of members, donors or target groups
with respect to the radical economic changes needed. This may mean
losing some members, but this is unavoidable and healthy. (Though
I should add that it is worth minimising such losses and that it takes
skill to do so. 'C'est le ton qui fait la musique!' or 'It's not what you
do, it's the way that you do it!') People who produce cars, pesticides,
etc. and are at the same time warm supporters of the protection of
rhinos or of Greenpeace, must at last be confronted with this ambi-
guity and hypocrisy.

It is now important for environmental groups to become more
aware of their stance towards society, economics and people: their
position, interests etc. They can have nice, green goals, but if they
don't get the support of many people, they will not get far. Environmentalists should become more politically and culturally aware, i.e.

aware of some history and of socio-economic backgrounds; they should be more sympathetic to the prisoner position of most people, and realise their own 'remoteness' from normal life and work, and their often more privileged position – by education, by having fewer direct responsibilities – than the bus conductor, the bank manager, the telephone repair person, the director of Novachem Ltd....

In the Netherlands, environmental and nature organisations have recently joined forces for public days of action. The groups forming this National Environment Action Coalition have drawn up a list of ten basic demands (on waste, traffic, energy etc.) and taken these out into the street together, to inform the public, and to pressure public authorities everywhere and at all levels. (One of the frustrations in this country is the strong recommendations in the official report 'Concern for Tomorrow' and the subsequent weak policy proposals now being put forward by the Dutch government.)

I am well aware that most of my examples are taken from the Netherlands. I'm sure that there are numerous similar and better examples and achievements in many other countries. I would be grateful for information on these (not only initiatives in the environmental field, but also social and cultural experiments and achievements), with a view to a second edition of my 'UTOPICS – a Catalogue of Alternatives': the Book of Hope!

Epilogue

Not as businessmen or trades unionists, nor as craftsmen or scientists, can we overcome our present problems, but only as human beings, only as people transcending their partial interests. This can probably only be done in a vast upsurge of mutual support, a joint movement working towards further human emancipation and awareness.

To turn round Adam Smith's well-known words: "It is no longer from the self-interest of the butcher, the brewer or the baker that our children can expect their dinner, but from their benevolent regard to the public interest and the future."

Benevolent? It is increasingly necessary; and they will be compelled to it by the force of increasingly dramatic circumstances. It is their self-interest better understood, to return to Smith!

Producers, craftsmen and tradesmen – as well as scientists, technicians and countless other workers – have to liberate themselves from the money-must-grow system and the overheated competition it gives rise to. So that they can, at last, act as responsible entrepreneurs and citizens. Many consumers, wage slaves, unemployed and other people will join in.

This would mean an economic revolution. An evolution would be preferable, but, in view of the short time left by nature before it collapses to a level hostile to humans, we shall have to trigger off a *revolutionary process* – wisely, calmly but firmly. It will probably take centuries rather than decades.

Guts, sweat and tears. But also the joy of cooperating, improvising and tasting the fruits of endurance. As the Borderlands sing: 'Rejoice, regreen, repair – shrink, shovel and share!'

It is a long way yet to 'Mens nova in terra sana', to a new spirit on a healthy Earth. A long way to a new paradigm. But it is in essence a 'liberation gaialogy', for which many stepping stones have already been laid all over the world.

It is also an exercise in intelligence, of trying to close Pandora's box which we smart alecs have opened too wide. An exercise in trying to get a grip on processes which are ruling us from way above our heads and leading us to the abyss.

Perhaps the saving grace of the dramatic, possibly already irreversible deterioration of our environment is that only a menace of such magnitude is capable of generating enough momentum for change.

The challenge now facing humankind – the transition from a growth economy to a steady-state economy – *is certainly greater than that faced by our ancestors in their evolution from hunters and gatherers to farmers.*

Homo faber trying at last to become homo sapiens.

Human beings becoming humanity...

We can still turn our Earth into a magnificent planet!

Some Facts and Other Absurdities

In California, more electric power is used annually than in the whole of Brazil.

Global annual expenditure on the military surpasses the total debts of the Third World.

In the Netherlands, acidification, caused partly by too many farm animals, already damages agricultural yields themselves to the tune of half a billion dollars a year.

Hydro-electric dams may well ruin more (photosynthesised) joules than they produce electrical ones.

Certainly modern agriculture uses more calories (oil, chemicals, fertiliser, machines) than it produces.

On our globe, in that thin 'life-peel' we call the biosphere, there are currently some 500 million cars in use, with some 1900 models to choose from.

Said Dutch Shell director: "We can't forbid the Chinese to buy cars." (And petrol, he must have thought.) "And who knows," he added, "the Earth might benefit from three degrees more warmth." (Mr van Engelshoven, Trouw, 3-3-89)

The proteins produced by the Third World farmer and fisherman, often not well-fed themselves, are being used by the First World to feed its pets. Daily, at least 1 million kilos are for instance being fed to 3 million Dutch cats and dogs...

In most 'rich' countries so much dirt and faeces is discharged into the waters that a whole industry has had to be developed to take it out again. One of the numerous examples of end-of-the-pipe intelligence.

Much modern food is defibred. To supplement our diet, these fibres have become an additional commodity. Double profit, taken from the consumer's purse.

Holland, rich in water, suffers from ...dehydration. The ground-water table is being lowered so as to allow ever heavier agricultural machines onto the land, ever sooner after winter.

In the same watery country, the last otter died several years ago because of pollution and lack of space. Now they want to import new otters from elsewhere, as they have already done with Polish beavers, transferred to the Biesbosch delta near Rotterdam, which is fed with tritium by the river Meuse. Aren't there more elegant ways of vivisection?

In Western Europe, the amount of agro-businessed butter and milk powder in the storehouses is sometimes so great that it is fed to calves – removed from their mothers. If their mothers could see this, they would be appalled – or would they think that man's intelligence is superior to theirs?

Modern means of communication and the mass media are less for mediation and communication than they are downright producers of a one-way, increasingly capital-intensive influence. Another 'tragedy of the commons'...

Many pesticides that are banned in the industrialised nations, nevertheless continue to be produced there and exported. They return partly in the cash crops from the Third World.

Vast amounts of money (and hence labour, technology, energy, natural resources and inventiveness) are spent on the military. Whereas what we want to defend so eagerly is rotting away under our feet.

Our modern society is one in which you should remain ill, otherwise the doctors are out of work; you should keep on smoking, otherwise the tobacco companies are out of work; etc.

The sun, which has served as Earth's sole source of energy for several billion years, has now been classified as 'alternative'.

Ivan Illich has calculated that the car, taking into account how many hours the owner has to work extra in order to be able to buy and use it, does not go faster than the bike.

Because oil is much too cheap, many a rich country is – to name but one example – neglecting its orchards and importing cheaper fruit from far away.

'Far away' then becomes dependent on this situation, and neglects in turn its own local production. (The same is caused by mass tourism.)

Due to commercialisation, pardon: privatisation, big businesses in Britain now own the water springing from the earth on people's private land.

In Germany, people can choose between 550 models of vacuum cleaner. Annually, 9 million such machines are sold in that country. (By the way, how many of the casts-off's could simply be repaired?)

Farmer A is modern, farmer B is old-fashioned (or really modern). Farmer A uses more input and has more output. He exhausts and poisons the soil, earns more, may even get more state subsidy than B, is able to buy more land and pushes B out of the market. B, who worked without ruining the soil, is expelled to the dole...

The agricultural exports of the Netherlands (including horticulture) are surpassed only by those of the USA and France. The animal fodder and other inputs for this small country's extremely intensive agriculture have been calculated to use an area, in other countries, equal to about three times its own agricultural acreage.

There was a man in the Dutch province of North Brabant who owned a wood. He was authorised to cut it and he sold it as timber. Then he gradually sold the earth and sand underneath and was authorised to fill the pit, as it developed, with refuse – an operation on which he earned too. Having got the space covered with earth again, he is now asking a public grant for ... planting trees.

Please continue

By making both the remuneration of capital and the organisation of employment flexible, the entrepreneur will be freed from the compulsion to continuous production and, at last, be able to care for the dogs.

NB. The continuous and full utilisation of a machine or a work force for the production of one (kind of) good or service may be advantageous at the micro level, but this may not be the case at all at the macro level.

Counter-arguments II*

Economists say it's the 'real economy', not money that generates growth. It's driven by travel and trade, by competition, by a growing population with new needs and desires, by scientific and technical development and creativity. Money is only following behind. If production and consumption didn't need money, it would be of no use and could never act as a driving force or a prime mover. Providers of money have no major influence.

To this I would reply that, in our society however, there's always something to buy, always something to lend and to invest. With its continuous consequences.

Moreover, and more importantly: *an effect may, in the course of time, develop into a co-cause, and from a co-cause into a main cause or even the main cause.*

Under which theoretical conditions, then, would it be possible for money – a mere means of exchange – to become a driving force? It should be a non-perishable means of exchange and the exclusive one, in a Market (see Note 7) where it reigns supreme (over land and labour, among others). There should be have-mores and have-lesses. It should have as its price itself, so that, by being used, its power can grow by accumulating. Additional money should be fairly easy to create, but certainly not by anyone. And last but not least, the economy – indeed the whole of society – should turn into an all-encompassing growth system.

In the history of the rich countries, I think these conditions have gradually been brought about. How? By an interplay of factors, of which the money system itself has gradually moved to centre stage.

The 'real economy' has developed from a money mover into a growth machine, which constantly needs and 'devours' enormous amounts of money and which has been *partly or mainly manoeuvred into this situation by the money-must-grow system itself.*

Thus did I arrive at my heretical hypothesis: business needing money is caused by money needing business. There is not only addiction to growth, but even *compulsion to growth.* Therefore, production must be freed from the 'modern' money system in order to be controllable and beneficial again.

May further study explore the value of this hypothesis!

* For Counter-arguments I, see page 67.

Notes

1. Actually, to express the consumption of energy, raw materials and so on per capita of the population is incorrect when applied to highly industrialised countries, where the volume of production no longer stands in direct relation to the size of the populations. (The same applies for developing countries with respect to their exported cash crops.) Per capita measurement is all right for bread, houses, private cars and suchlike, but not for most other goods, many of which are exported. It reinforces the ideology of 'everything happens because the (domestic) consumer needs it'. Paul and Ann Ehrlich are too extreme in their use of the per capita calculation, I feel. "Every American baby will consume ...etc." (In 'The Population Explosion.') Supposing the USA had only 50 million inhabitants, each citizen could then have three cars, two houses, one boat, one helicopter, etc. and pollute as much as they do now with 230 million.

2. It is reported that in the United States, for example, the total wealth of the country's multi-millionaires is roughly equal to all the money saved at commercial banks by the population as a whole... "It's a rich man's world", as Abba sang.

3. In (Islamic) countries where interest is forbidden, as was the case in early Christianity, the money-lender is rewarded rather like our shareholders, i.e. with property shares.

4. By the way, a surplus trade balance (i.e. with exports exceeding imports) necessarily means that another country or other countries have a negative trade balance! (See also Note 38.) Equally, receiving interest or dividend or making excess profits means that it is taken from elsewhere, paid for by other (often hard-working!) people.

5. As regards exponential (explosive) growth – 1, 2, 4, 8, etc. – this should be distinguished from calmer, linear growth: 1, 2, 3, etc. Ongoing reinvestments of dividend and interest (simple and compound) generate exponential production growth.

   To quote Kenneth Boulding, the inventor of the term 'spaceman-economy' which should replace the present 'cowboy-economy': "Anyone who believes that exponential growth can go on forever in a finite world is either a madman or an economist."

6. Perhaps it is not too speculative to suggest that, in previous centuries, democracy was allowed to develop because the money system protected vested interests. (As for Ford's saying, the source is unknown to me. In less strong words, see 'Motto' in Ford News, March 1, 1922.)

7. Karl Polanyi – Daly & Cobb (1989) remind us – distinguishes between market and Market: the traditional, region-based market and the modern market. (Perhaps we could similarly distinguish money from Money: money for exchange, for regulating and for undertakings large or small, on the one hand; and Power Capital (often external), on the other.) Polanyi draws attention to the great transformation of nature into land, life into labour and patrimony into capital.

As for the Industrial Revolution, it is usually considered to be Manna from Heaven, as an important step forward in producing wealth and employment. However, this ignores the crucial fact that in previous centuries land reforms had already ousted the larger part of the population from their land and livelihood. The farmers had been robbed of soil and tools, of home and meaningfulness and turned into an urban proletariat. All this occurred by the same process of capital gaining ever greater hold on production, and pushing it up, which later gave birth to the Industrial Revolution. This surge of industrial development was in fact partly a kind of repair of the enormous damage caused previously.

8. Investments in property (land, buildings) have the same forcing effect.

9. In the case of extremely expensive undertakings, countries, universities or businesses do join forces. Examples include: fast breeder nuclear reactors (Kalkar, Malville), nuclear fusion research, space research, the airbus. This only makes the question the more urgent and pertinent: how much can we yet afford to waste through widespread, massive and intensive competition? Hence my feelings as regards competition differ somewhat from Daly's.

10. I sometimes wonder whether the notion of Original Sin has not to do with our ancestors' awareness not only of death but also of entropy. An awareness of entropy and the related notions of over- and underdevelopment may well provide a material basis for developing a general feeling about a global 'togetherness' and interdependence of the Earth's peoples.

Authors like Jeremy Rifkin and Georgescu-Roegen seem to pay little attention to the happy phenomenon of neg-entropy – the ordering and the evolution of life – preferring mainly to stress the process of decay.

Ill. Nel van Koten

11. For simplicity's sake, I am ignoring the now very marginal, though probably older, kinds of rudimentary life (worms and so on) living by means of chemosynthesis on the ocean bed near sulphur wells.

12. The terms 'shallow environmentalism' and 'deep ecology' are from the Norwegian philosopher Arne Naess. A more colourful image: light green and dark green.

Part of the environmental movement is 'shallow' in its attempt to be realistic, to act as an understanding partner in discussions with government and industry. It supports the high-speed train, 'cleaner' cars and across-the-board application of eco-technology, leaving untouched production volumes and keeping people blind to the basic absurdity of present-day 'productivism', mobility and their wealth in general. Wolfgang Sachs, commenting on the (old?) approach of the World Watch Institute: "The ecological crisis should be met with a 'virtue of enoughness', not with the gospel of efficient resource management."

13. To think is difficult. We tend to swing from one extreme to the other, without realising that reality is complex and the truth can be perceived in myriad different ways, formed by thousands of opinions and experiences. Or we are in favour of one pole and defend it by comparing it with its atrocious opposite – often too simple a way out. We also have difficulty thinking in terms of processes; we tend to consider reality in terms of stable, set forms, although this is hardly ever the case. Moreover, our reductionist thinking stands in the way of wider (more 'holistic') approaches. And we gallop away in ideas, idealism and psychology, easily forgetting the underlying material – economic and physical – situation. Or we have difficulty in seeing that an initially good process can, by continuing, turn sour. Finally, we all have our prejudices – fixations on own experiences which we tend to generalise, and hobbyhorses we enjoy riding (like the money-must-grow system!).

Be that as it may, it is often wise to stop thinking and start doing...

14. The Keynesian approach 'avant la lettre', something Marx had not at all foreseen, I think. In fact, better wages boil down to a 'simple' extension of the money circulation. An extension can be made by increasing the money volume, but the speed of circulation also plays a role. (It should be noted here that, because of the many basic financial obligations of life (food, rent, etc.), the greater part of an average wage does not remain for long under the control of the person who earned it.)

As for the improvement of the conditions of the working class, this was a battle won not only by the Socialists, but furthered also, partly on ethical grounds, by Christians and Liberals. An important factor was the need of business owners to have a better and healthier workforce at their disposal. It is often difficult to distinguish ethical from (hidden) economic reasons. Ethical demands frequently arise when it is economically desirable and feasible to meet them. (I am afraid the individual human psyche does not behave very differently, often hiding underlying motives...)

15. For simplicity's sake I here bypass the Fourth World: the relatively poor and non-participating people in the rich countries. It is rather false to point out the poverty in, say, Nepal to someone on the dole in a rich Northern country. They say it's better for everyone to be poor than to be poor amidst many wealthier people.

16. It is amazing how easy it always is for investors to rally trades unions, politicians and public authorities for their projects with the carrot of employment. They always stress job creation, not profit creation. Whereas, after a while, the new company automates its operations and needs less personnel. Then, on behalf of the dismissed workers, new businesses will be promoted and welcomed! The spiral again.

    NB. A magic concept is 'labour or worker productivity' (productive output per labourer). This, we learn, should increase all the time. What it basically boils down to in practice is an unending process of business automation – a process driven by competition and favoured by the fact that (in the rich, industrialised countries) a labour force is more expensive than most other forms of energy. Taking into account that many workers who have lost their job stay on the dole for quite some time or even until the age of final retirement, one can say that the increase of worker productivity means: greater consumption of energy, natural resources, machines and chemicals, hence further deterioration of the environment.

    By the way, fighting our alienation also means checking the use of terms and the meaning they have acquired. I have already mentioned the 'per capita' calculations, which may give a wrong impression. There is also the 'want' of, or 'desire' for energy, transport, etc., which in reality is the *need* for such things. We talk of 'privatisation', which is in fact commercialisation (cfm. Robertson). And so on.

17. This domination is also highly responsible for the fact that labour is heavily taxed in comparison with other forms of energy (oil, coal, etc.). This favours automation, as pointed out. Workers have to pay insurance premiums to cover unemployment benefits, while it is cheap fuel (much too cheap from the ecological point of view) which leads to them being replaced by machines and chemical processes!

18. Herman Daly reminds us that Adam Smith emphasised in his 'Theory of Moral Sentiments' that the market is a system so dangerous that it presupposes the moral force of shared community values as its necess-

ary restraining context. (There couldn't be a better one-sentence sum-
mary of his and Cobb's recent book 'For the Common Good'!)

In earlier writings (1980), Daly introduced the image of the Invisible
Foot, the counterpart of Adam Smith's Invisible Hand. By this, Daly
points to all the costs ignored by the market system: the 'external dis-
economies'.

NB. For readers not familiar with Smith: he believed that every individual was 'continually exerting himself to find out the most advantageous
employment for whatever capital he can command.' 'It is not from the
benevolence of the butcher, the brewer or the baker that we expect
our dinner, but from their regard to their own interest.' Each producer
'intends only his own security; and by directing that industry in such a
manner as its produce may be of the greatest value, he intends only his
own gain, and he is in this, as in many other cases, led by an invisible
hand to promote an end which was no part of his intention. Nor is it
always the worse for the society that it was no part of it. By pursuing
his own interest he frequently promotes that of society more effectually
than when he really intends to promote it. I have never known much
good done by those who affected to trade for the public good. It is an
affectation, indeed, not very common among merchants, and very few
words need be employed in dissuading them from it'. ('The Wealth of
Nations', Modern Library, New York, 1937, p. 421, 14 and 423) This
appears to be a sound reaction to Christian paternalism by which the
rich should care for the poor. On the other hand, I believe Smith
makes the businessman stick to a kind of animal or primitive instinct
rather than helping him to develop to become a member of society
with wider responsiblities. (NB I apologise. Many animals and primi-
tives behave more wisely and socially than modern humans!)

As regards the Invisible Hand, it comes to mind that nature works in
rather the same way. A year with more mice means more offspring for
the owl population, but in later years with less mice, the owls may get
into serious trouble. Is this one of the indications that we humans
should make an evolutionary effort to use our brains and invent something better than relying on 'blind' market forces?

19. This example shows at the same time that a want or demand often
tends to be more of a real need, a necessity. Someone who, because
the city was full, at last finds a flat in a dormitory town is forced to use
more transport. By taking the elevator to his/her flat on the 6th floor,
he/she uses more energy, etc. Yet we speak of 'our demand' for transport, energy, etc. as if we act out of choice, out of free will.

Of course, if we raise the temperature in our house, it's our own
doing. But much of the increase in 'our demand for energy' etc., as it

is called, is simply forced upon us. (For instance by building badly insulated houses!)

20. Following this line of thought, the same environmentalists also commonly stress the importance of other consumer behaviour, in the household, etc. However valuable these changes in lifestyle may be, though, they should not obscure the need for structural changes. In fact, a person's contribution to the destruction of the environment should be measured less by the number of bottles dropped in the recycling container or the use of the train instead of the car than by the extent of his/her participation in the money system (property, shares, savings, mortgage, level of expenses)! And a person's contribution to saving the environment should be measured less by the way he/she keeps the house than by how they are contributing to structural changes, public education, etc.

21. A university teacher, for instance, may have less difficulty in biking, using second-hand chairs, storing his/her books on old shelves, etc. than a manual worker whose work provides less satisfaction and status and for whom goods are the only materialisation and manifestation of his/her daily, subordinated routine work.

22. One of the merits of Aristotle was his recognition that it is difficult to distinguish exactly where an economic activity changes from good to bad and to distinguish between a useful (natural) and a useless (unnatural) activity.

The Greek 'chrèmatistikè' means the normal acquisition of goods, but it can turn into harmful money-making. "The acquisition of goods is of two kinds; one, which is necessary and approved of, is to do with household-management. The other is to do with trade and depends on exchange. (...) This is not productive of goods in the full sense but only through their exchange. And it is thought to be concerned with coinage (...) It is due to this that there is thought to be no limit to wealth or property. Because it closely resembles that [first] form of acquisition of goods, many suppose that the two are one and the same. But they are not the same, though admittedly they are not very different; one is natural, the other is not. (...) One is limited, the other is not [its end is sheer increase] (...and) is justly regarded with disapproval, since it arises not from nature but from men's gaining from each other. (...) Some people therefore imagine that increase is the function of household-management, and never cease to believe that their store of coined money ought to be either hoarded, or increased without limit."
(The Politics, 1258a38, 1256b40&41, 1258a14 and 1257b25. Penguin Classics, 1981)

23. 'Words ought to be a little wild, for they are the assault of thoughts

upon the unthinking.' A beautiful saying by Keynes which opens the recent book by Daly and Cobb.

24. Depending on one's definition of capitalism, one could make a further distinction, i.e. between capitalism and money-making. And between profit-making and money-making. And surely one should distinguish even these from profiteering.

25. John Griffith, Chancellor of Manchester University: "The 50 years after 1830 saw an outburst of government legislation reforming the franchise, the municipalities and the poor law, the police and prisons; and regulating employment and hours of work, public health, schools, housing, many particular trades, diseases in cattle, the conduct of fairs, railways and joint stock companies, sale of food and drugs, pawnbrokers, pharmacists and medics. Hundreds of Acts of Parliament created the regulatory State, which Professor A.V. Dicey, at the beginning of this century, called collectivism, and which, he said, involved two assumptions: the denial that laisser faire was generally a principle of sound legislation, and the belief in the benefit of governmental guidance or interference, even when it greatly limited the sphere of individual choice or liberty. (...) Until quite recently," Griffith goes on, "there was a reference point called *the public interest*. Politicians spoke of it with respect even when they were disregarding it. More importantly, civil servants and local government officers believed in it and many spent their lives in its pursuit. They saw themselves as the guardians of the common good by which they evaluated and often resisted the demands of powerful interest groups. (...) Today, collectivism and the pursuit of the common good are devalued." (The Guardian, 14-6-90)

26. As is well known, although shareholders may legally be the owners of a company, they often have little say about the course along which it is steered. However, they still have the power to take back their money. In turn, to protect themselves against this eventuality, companies create defensive holdings or major financial reserves of their own. In some years, rich companies earn more on their own capital investments than on their products. (Therefore, they are less interested in changing the money system than smaller companies that depend on external financing. An important point for a strategy of change.)

27. "...l'énorme surplomb d'un secteur financier proliférant qui recouvre de son ombre l'économie réelle et menace de l'étouffer." (Le Monde, 23-12-86, Paul Fabra)

28. Rather than turn the Houses of Parliament into a dunghouse, as William Morris suggests in 'News from Nowhere', it would be better to transform option markets and many other financial businesses whose usefulness is not always evident, into, say, urban recycling centres, giv-

ing our smart financial yuppies an opportunity to do some useful work at last...

Daly and Cobb list some modern 'chrematists' (money-makers) as follows: litigious lawyers, tax-gimmicky accountants, merger manipulators, greenmailers, junk-bond dealers, and unproductive rent-seekers of all kinds.

Finally, Keynes on speculation: "Speculators may do no harm as bubbles on a steady stream of enterprise. But the position is serious when enterprise becomes the bubble on a whirlpool of speculation." ('The General Theory'.)

29. When we shake our pitying and pedantic heads at their long queues in front of half-empty shops, we should remember that the USSR is, or was until recently, the largest producer of oil, gas, steel (twice as much as the USA), zinc and nickel in the world.

PART TWO

30. To introduce yet another image – always useful for educational purposes: Daly compares a growth economy with an aeroplane that can't remain stationary in the air, whereas a helicopter (the steady-state economy) can, and can even fly backwards.

31. Nuclear energy, dams for hydro-electricity, end-of-pipe health care, Concorde, overscaled traffic facilities, etc. By the way, the circumstance that the usual 'solutions' are becoming defective means that *the basis for change becomes material*: a crucial circumstance when time demands the start of a pre-revolutionary phase. Revolution? (Nothing to do with guillotines or Stalinists!) What else does the making of a Great U-turn boil down to? And I am thinking in terms of centuries, rather than decades. Unfortunately, for the sake of nature – our real and only 'cork' – we have to hurry up. This is the field of tension in which environmentalists have to work: on the one hand patience with people and structures, on the other urgency for nature's sake...

32. In some countries environmentalists have listed green alternatives in 'hopeful' catalogues. A broad variety, including such seemingly remote subjects – but necessary for convival – as education, building, health care, money, control and community work can already be found in the Dutch booklet 'Utopics – een catalogus van alternatieven' (1980).

33. In Davis, California (40,000 inhabitants) a number of alternatives have been put into practice *together*, thus setting off a whole 'green' culture. Bikes have priority over cars. Houses are built so as to save energy and have solar collectors. Lawns are replaced by vegetable gardens (pes-

ticides prohibited). Rubbish is collected in four separate lots, enabling much to be sold to recycling firms, for the benefit of the community budget. The weekly fresh-food market is also quite new for a country used to frozen food, as is the annual second-hand clothes market. Do-it-yourself-arts are being promoted. The meetings of the town council are open to the public whose comments and suggestions are instantly considered. Davis has set a limit to its growth: 50,000 people. It has the lowest unemployment and crime rates of the USA, and TV consumption is half the average. The energy saving achieved is 60%. Already a second and a third town are planned because the population flocks to live there. (See Richard St. George, 'No Mean City', in *Resurgence* No. 134)

34. Let's recall Henry Ford's saying about the money system, the understanding of which would cause a general stir. There is also, for instance, a movement in Germany and Switzerland (inspired by the 'money circulist' – my term. W.H. – Silvio Gesell, who is favourably quoted by Keynes) which advocates a system of liberal enterprise that is freed not only from communism but also from capitalism. It is focused mainly on the wrongness of interest and it propagates Free Money.

In order to stimulate the circulation of money while preventing interest from encouraging unwanted accumulations, Gesell invented a system of negative interest. People had to buy stamps which were to be stuck on the banknotes they did not spend quickly enough. (This was successfully practised in the Austrian town Wörgl, after World War I, but the government, which holds the monopoly over money, put an end to it.) Modern Gesellians propose that demand deposits, which today are the main form of money, should be taxed.

There are also the followers of Henry George who focus on land and want to tax land rather than labour. (Compare this with the idea of a basic tax on energy, currently advocated by many environmentalists.)

I should comment that, even without interest, the profit system will ensure full continuation of capital accumulation and therefore of the domination by Big Money and of its role of pushing up production. I don't know whether the whole institution of interest can be used as an instrument with which to achieve sufficient change in the present economy.

Some of the supporters of interest-free money are just those business-people who wish to do more and cheaper business. The same thing applies to the barter system which in itself is surely better than, through trading, accumulating outside 'power capital'.

Opponents of cheap money believe that it is harmful, because a wider and faster circulation of money engenders more activity and more production. This was desirable in times of depression (Keynes!), but has now become highly undesirable, except for the production of green and social services. Modern green 'circulists' want to correct this by ecotaxing. This may well be a viable path. (Surely, in economically stagnating localities and regions, the injection of some money, like oil in a machinery, can be wholesome – as examples from all over the world have shown and continue to show.)

Anyway, the value of Gesellians, Georgians and others (anthroposophists, for instance) is to stimulate the discussion about interest, land taxation, and the ways and use of money – a theme which, as Hans Binswanger (professor of economics at the Technical University of Sankt Gallen) states, our societies have catapulted far away.

35. As far as energy is concerned, it is clear that in a saner economy its production will be low and it will be used in an intelligent, 'neg-entropic' (non-wasteful) way. The use of coal, oil and gas should be minimised (and counterbalanced by vast reforestation). Nuclear power is to be abandoned altogether. (One could, however, make a distinction between careful research – i.e. research that can be stopped at any moment – and dangerous production, pushed by capital investments and used for the firing of run-away economies...)

So-called realists will say that we can't do without these energy sources if we are to preserve our Light Age existence.

The output of the renewable sources is low and will never be able to meet the needs of our societies loaded with hamburgers, rockets and private cars. However, in a society with a considerably reduced level of production – by 60% we ventured – that output will represent a much greater fraction of the new, vastly lowered needs for energy.

Moreover, entropy-conscious environmentalists will point out that the value of renewable energy sources is precisely their...weakness!

By the way, the world's main problems will not concern energy, but too much u.v. radiation and the lack of fresh water.

36. Current satisfaction about, say, the recycling and energy saving now being achieved by municipalities and in production processes is a severe obstacle to furthering awareness about the massive pruning back that is actually necessary. In the European environmental movement, a discussion is going on between followers of André Gorz and Joseph Huber on the one hand and those of Otto Ullrich on the other. One could say it is a discussion between light and dark green environmentalists. Is the way out of our problems via 'ecological modernisation' of the present production system (Gorz, Huber) or is it via a more radical split with this system by means of de-industrialisation (Ullrich)? The Brundtland report 'Our Common Future' is based on technological

optimism – the official ideology of big business – and was understandably supported, in the U.N. Commission on Environment and Development that prepared it, by the many Third World countries trapped by the economic status quo.

Since 1970 when we started the pressure group Aktie Strohalm, my friends and I have embraced 'deep ecology' as opposed to 'shallow environmentalism'. Combined with a solid analysis of the financial and industrial powers, we have always tended towards what can now be called the Ullrich line. As we put it: 'We need large-scale limitations and small-scale developments.' This means limiting what is too big and over-centralised and developing what is optimally-scaled and decentralised (cfm. the Dutch eco-philosopher Pieter Schroevers and the well-known E.F. Schumacher, to mention two 'shrink pioneers'). 'No' to nuclear power and new high-speed trains, and a reduction of production volumes and mobility; and 'yes' to wind turbines, bicycles, normal-scale organic farming, normal public transport, etc.

37. Good environmental education may well start from trivial subjects and activities, but progresses along stepping stones to further awareness, to wider activity, both socially and politically. Environmental education should not just be concentrated on children learning about plants and animals. In the rich countries, the adult town dweller should learn about cars and entropy, about water pollution and organic food; about economics and over-development; and about how to participate in activities and decision-making. Moreover, environmental education must anticipate. It should always put in focus the long term, the wider perspective; and should combine concrete, short-term steps with the long-term objective. Such anticipative education will pave the way for the more severe Earth-protective measures that are certainly yet to come. The main aim of environmental education should be to combat the general alienation from nature and from what is really good for us. This education should therefore always be slightly subversive, beneficially subversive. And, above all, it should make people self-reliant and self-confident, and equip them for helping to reshape society.

To see how information and education campaigns can be organised to be less of a one-way activity, see 'Media' in Part III.

38. There is something to be said against autarchy or the economic self-suffiency of countries. The opposite is interdependency through division of labour (i.e. of production) and trade even in vital products. (NB. This is the way Big Money organises our economies and the whole world; and it also happens to be considered, for instance in socialist thinking, an important step in the development of the forces of production and therefore of humanity in general...)

This economic interdependency enables nations or corporations to influence one another or to put joint pressure to bear upon a single country. Consider economic sanctions against countries which tend to practise tyranny or apartheid, or which continue to damage the ozone layer, build dangerous dams or cut down forests – activities which damage the soil and the world's climate.

People like James Robertson seem to aim at self-reliance rather than at self-sufficiency. In view of the ecological carrying capacity, the energy consumption and the vulnerability of our economies, I think trade must be very much reduced everywhere, and I therefore strive for as much self-sufficiency as possible. It may also reduce the risk of war and other threats which now arise over foreign natural resources and markets which have become vital to our present economic system.

The subject is not easy. In history, man (or the leading man) has shown himself as rather exploring and expanding. Is pleading for self-sufficiency a silly, backward attitude? I used to make a comparison between nations (or regions) and individuals; the more we ourselves are able to function on our own, the better we can establish sound relations with others!

Daly and Cobb (1990) envisage 'balanced' trade, to be achieved through import quotas and capital immobility – the latter because capital now moves easily to the cheap-labour countries, thus impoverishing the working population of the country left, while switching the new country to 'cash production' for foreign markets.

They remind us of Keynes' idea on the subject: "I sympathize, therefore, with those who would minimize, rather than with those who would maximize, economic entanglement between nations. Ideas, knowledge, art, hospitality, travel – these are the things which should of their nature be international. But let goods be homespun whenever it is reasonably and conveniently possible; and above all, let finance be primarily national."

Daly and Cobb: "Balanced trade and capital immobility imply each other. (...) The consequence of free international finance (a necessary complement to free trade) has been the running up of unrepayable debts. Large surplus accumulations of money resulting from trade imbalances sought ways to grow exponentially and to recycle back to the deficit country to finance further trade deficits. (...) Like international trade, international borrowing and lending [in their view to be greatly curtailed and only for clearly beneficial and productive projects] should be between nations as communities, not between subnational entities seeking only their private interests." And they add: "This is an area for further reflection and research." (p.231 and 233)

39. Without overdoing this as in some convivial or socialist experiments.
Here again: 'Est modus in rebus'. But in adult education centres and
schools I have seen (to mention only one example of work differentia-
tion) admirable lessons being given by ordinary, blue-collar workers.
By means of the variation of work, we could also divide our time
between small-scale work and large-scale, intensive production. The
conveyor belt will certainly remain necessary, because it is efficient for
many types of production.
The proposed 'flexibilisation' of the work force (in my view all of us!)
should not be confused with the way employers currently tend to treat
personnel, that is, increasingly giving only temporary contracts.

40. In response to the present desire in Eastern European countries for an
absolutely free market, Galbraith has pointed out that the Western system has already been considerably corrected and is in fact a rather
regulated market economy. (*The Guardian*, December 1989.)

41. Daly and Cobb refer to 'person-in-community' to mark the difference
from the modern 'individual'. To balance current over-individualisation, and as an environmentalist who puts first things first, I would, in
these terms, rather suggest as a central concept: 'community-with-
people' or 'community-of-people'. Ecologically and economically, the
individual is, to say it 'wildly', nothing; he/she only exists in relation
to, and in mutual dependence with, thousands of other individuals.
And with millions of plants and animals. (Think of where your food
comes from, and your clothes; your house, your water and energy.
How many people have contributed to them?) With some exaggeration to balance, I sometimes consider the individual to be a delusion,
developed by and in economies favouring disintegration and supported
by honest liberalism and by religions grown so 'vertically' that they
have catapulted God away from the Earth into Heaven, only linked
with humans through very individual and very thin kite strings....
Of course, those just awakening from a dictatorial nightmare, as currently in Eastern Europe, will prefer 'person-in-community' or will
even embrace the Western orientation solely towards the 'individual'.
But my expectation is that, after emotions have calmed down and in-
sight developed, in those countries too, people will generally appreciate
at least the notion of 'person-in-community'.

42. Herman Daly suggests (1980) that a kind of annual auction of depletion
quotas should be applied to energy and materials. But I wonder
whether this would not, under the present circumstances, only favour
those possessing most capital (big companies, funds), who may not follow – or be able to follow – the path we ought to take in order to
survive. I do not know Daly's present ideas on this matter.

As for his 'minimum sacrifice of personal freedom': I guess the environmental catastrophe will require tremendous sacrifices, not in the least at the personal level.

While completing the text of this book, I have managed to read parts of Daly's new book 'For the Common Good'. I can now add, therefore, that I believe he has stuck to this idea. I am afraid that the richer corporations, by buying the quotas, will continue to influence and create the demand for their products. From the ecological point of view, this is not an assurance that production will go in the right direction. In my view, maintaining wide competition, as Daly favours, is also an approach that may put or keep people on the wrong foot. I fear that too much waste, by double work, will be the ongoing result. Would ecotaxing be able to provide enough steerage in the highly competitive market place?

As to the subject of planning or free enterprise, Daly points out that one either has the market economy and profit-making, or state bureaucracy with every worker being an employee. You can't reject both profit-making and central planning. 'If one dislikes centralised bureaucratic decision-making then one must accept the market and the profit motive, if not as a positive good then as the lesser of two evils.' (p. 48/49) It depends, I think, on what one calls centralised planning and profit-making. A fair entrepreneurial reward is different from a profit which surpasses the role of an incentive. Moreover, do we envisage a context of competition which compels businesses to make continual large profits in order to defend themselves?

As for central planning, are clipping the wings of capitals and fixing (annual) depletion quotas, for instance, not acts of considerably centralised decision-making? Moreover, what is so dangerous about a town council disposing of a few millions and deciding on granting a starter loan to a health food shop or an amusement arcade (see following note)? Could such a decision not be taken a) quickly, and b) 'in the open'? And is the green shopkeeper not consequently entering into normal business competition with other health food shops? And would there be a difference in paying back that loan if it were from the municipality rather than from a bank? (By the way, why not have the banks be represented on the municipal funding committee? Sound advice is always useful! They could even administer the funds.)

While apologising for extending this long note, let us take a quick glance at the ideas of Daly and Cobb concerning taxes since it is a subject which I myself have not given much thought to: "In the ideal scheme all the means of raising public funds would also function as means of attaining public goals. Income, gift and inheritance taxes would be retained for their redistributive effects. Taxes designed to internalize costs would become a large element in this ideal system. Tariffs would insure national control of the national economy. The auctioning of rights to mine or severance taxes on the use of scarce resources could set a scale for the economy as a whole. Excise and gasoline taxes would discourage use of harmful substances or make scarce resources available for more primary and production needs. The land tax would end speculation in land, encourage socially beneficial use, and recover for the community unearned profits. Users fees would cover the costs of the services provided." (p.330)

43. The resistance of entrepreneurs to restrictions is both understandable and overcomable. Building contractors in Davis, California, confronted with the energy-saving requirements set by the town council, were at first fiercely opposed, but have since turned into state-wide advocators of the new type of housing. Many new expensive techniques, which enterprises have had to adopt because of environmental protection laws, have later proved to yield saleable goods or services.

Daly reminds us of a restriction in force in the 19th century. Competing shipowners often overloaded their ships, which resulted in naval disasters. The English MP Samuel Plimsoll therefore suggested, in 1875, a load limitation for each ship. The shipowners were fiercely opposed. Yet, his law was passed and limitations were accepted, first for all British ships, later internationally. A similar limitation should now be introduced for our economies, in order to stop overloading our ecosystems. (Herman Daly, interview NRC-Handelsblad 18-6-89).

44. A friend of mine wanted to start a health-food shop, but the bank, whom he had asked for support, tried to persuade him instead to start yet another amusement arcade ... Organically grown carrots or one-armed bandits – which would you like to offer our youngsters?

45. A more 'liberal' (or private) way would be what a bank in a run-down quarter of Chicago started to do. It repumped its money into the neighbourhood instead of supporting outside ventures with higher returns, as is usually done. Now the area has apparently embarked on an upward spiralling path. (Jonathon Porritt mentioned this in his TV-series 'Where on Earth are we going?'.) The Grameenbank in Bangladesh is conducting a similar 'social-keynesian' undertaking and is only lending money to the very poor, with amazingly positive results, it seems. But these activities hinge simply on individual bankers getting new ideas. One can't even expect many others to do likewise because of their clients/savers and other factors and influences (like the orders from the bank's head office) requiring the highest and/or safest possible revenue.

46. The social-utopian Charles Fourier (France, early 19th century) pro-
ceeds from the idea that people don't usually like to work and that the
motivation to do so should be rooted in our 'passions'. In his co-
operatives ('phalanstères'), he suggested as an incentive fierce competition between the productive groups, with non-material rewards. Marquis Childs (to take a contemporary author) is a proponent of close-
knit labour-management cooperation and a heavy redistribution of income, together with dynamic free enterprise.

The Old Testament refers to the idea of a Jubilee Year. Every 50th
year the tribe would reallocate all possessions equally among its members. Then development would be unhindered for half a century, until
the next social reshuffle. Here again we have: macro-equity combined
with micro-diversification. The idea as such has probably never been
executed, but the purpose is clear.

As for our modern ecological crisis, we should not forget that only if
we are all more or less in the same boat materially will shrinkage operations, severe cuts and rationing be easier to accept than if we allow
major differences to remain between people, such as disparities in
wealth or in power.

The Belgian economist Ernest Mandel says that humans are not as
good as Jean-Jacques Rousseau thinks they are, nor as bad as the liberals and conservatives imagine. Mandel prefers to put humans 'on neutral'. The society they live in will draw the good or bad things out of
them.

Daly and Cobb comment on humankind's more social and brotherly
(sisterly) feelings: "We view them as analogous to weak muscles that
have atrophied from lack of use. Because they are weak it would not
be prudent to depend too much on them too soon. But rehabilitation
requires exercise, not tranquilised bed rest. While we generally advocate market-like arrangements, we certainly do not view the market as,
in T.S. Eliot's words, 'a system so perfect that no one needs to be
good'".

47. A link has been suggested with protestantism, which stresses the individual's own responsibility. Phenomena like nepotism and corruption
seem to develop easier in Latin countries than further up north. But
perhaps another reason is that in the Latin countries direct, warm
human relations have been sustained longer than in the north.

48. A main road to achieving change is through environmental education,
carried out and passed on by citizens themselves, combined with community activities and informative work within businesses, trades
unions, churches and women's organisations. All this – and more –
should be supported by 'structural' changes (e.g. the municipality starts

collecting waste in various separate categories, creates better biking facilities, etc.) and by the media. In the environmentally advanced countries, such education could be geared to vast governmental campaigns.
In some countries, like the Netherlands, the government is now promoting 'social renewal' – mainly intended for minorities having difficulty integrating with society and getting jobs. This operation could
well be broadened to all those who are currently working on the outer
edge of society or whose work is not as valued as it should be: housewives, volunteers, welfare and community workers and the like. 'Social
renewal' could be enlarged and intensified to contribute considerably
to the founding of the new economy.

49. In my view, doing some necessary work should also apply to people
who stay in a country temporarily (except for tourists who stay only a
short while). It is in fact highly alienating to travel around in a foreign
country with a full purse, taking from the land without returning more
than abstract money to it. Likewise, political and other refugees should
be employed creatively. My proposal for 'making everyone productive'
would make everyone participatory and useful, and decrease barriers
and irritation between people, especially between established inhabitants and newcomers, like immigrant groups; or between the rural
population and city people settling in the country. 'Everyone productive' would also limit in a natural, 'organic' way the amount of people
living and staying in a country or region.

50. Some leading environmentalists in developing countries point out that
writing off debts will not work if the government concerned is cor-
rupt, because such a step will immediately be followed by an attempt
to obtain new loans, most of which will again disappear. With regard
to these countries, these environmentalists plead for strict ecological
(and social) conditions for debt write-off.

51. To lure the military into this reconversion and into helping with this
huge global regreening enterprise, we could perhaps label it 'Operation
Desert Storm'...

52. A word about crime. State bureaucracy certainly generates corruption
and criminality, but the criminality developed under upscaled and glo-
balised capitalism isn't peanuts either. Increasing mobility, too free
capitalism (money-making) and disintegrating societies are just the right
mixture for today's criminality. It is becoming a serious threat to the
normal functioning of our economies and democracies. As for money,
a huge amount is circulating in the criminal circuits: 200 billion dollars
in the international drug trade alone (1989).
In a country like the Netherlands, it is estimated that Crime Inc. pulls

in some 20 billion dollars annually. Here is another 'material' reason
for authorities to start helping with the Great U-Turn!

PART THREE

53. Eating less meat refers to the wasteful conversion of vegetable protein
    to animal protein through animal farming on a massive scale. For meat
    requirements, agricultural land in South America and other regions is
    turned into huge ranches which are quickly overgrazed, depleted and
    destroyed. As for energy-saving at home, a simple tip concerns the use
    of the hay-box or sleeping bag for cooking: a dish, briefly boiled on
    the cooker in the morning, will slowly but surely be cooked in such a
    heat store by the time you want to eat it at night.
54. For most people, the territory towards which we feel a sense of pos-
    session and want to look after ends at the doorstep. Yet the street, the
    whole place, the whole country is ours! This feeling should be encour-
    aged, provided it goes with a sense of caring. Duties go hand in hand
    with rights. I hope a natural sense of responsibility will develop which
    largely surpasses the front door and goes beyond the rather nasty words
    'right' and 'duty'.
55. I can't resist a utopian note. In the long run we will have to change
    the whole school system, combining learning with some normal, adult-
    like work. (This appears to improve learning results and is an import-
    ant reason for an economy on a smaller scale, with more visible,
    human-powered activities). We need smaller classes and more part-
    time people to support the teachers; also more vertically structured age
    groups, with those who have learned something passing it on to
    younger pupils and thus digesting the teaching while practising some
    responsibility. In this way, they are not 'pupils' the whole time. Educa-
    tional experiments on these lines are being conducted in several coun-
    tries.
56. The reader may think: the author is never satisfied. That's right, but it
    doesn't mean set-ups like in Mondragon are not good. On the con-
    trary, they are valuable steps towards another economy. Under the
    present circumstances, without an overall change, without a change
    affecting the whole of society and world trade (hence my use of the
    word 'revolution'), no achievement is one hundred per cent successful.
    But they are or can be steps towards the future. For that purpose, they
    should and must keep the path open for further change. Perhaps even
    'Mondragon' has become too 'successful' as regards its energy use, its
    burden on the local and global ecosystems and its balance with the

Third World. You might then ask: do you want those people to return to the same poverty and unemployment they experienced thirty years ago? No, certainly not, of course. The great value of 'Mondragon' is that people themselves, with the help of a few pioneers, developed their town outside and despite mainstream economy and finance. But to develop genuine sustainability is yet another story ...

57. Daly & Cobb think *unlimited* inequality contradicts the very notion of community. Referring to the notion of 'confiscatory taxation', they write: "We think that eventually a healthy community might evolve in which a notion of this sort was politically acceptable." (p. 331)

58. Hence a prime task for our societies: how do we bring the 'aristoi' to the surface? How do we get the just, socially-minded, non-egoistical and really green people to be the new kind of managers, executives and officials, the new pioneers? The political parties, whether left or right, do not seem to have succeeded in this. Their second or third ranks often contain more of these people who remain in the twilight, in the dark even. The problem is that the 'aristoi' don't really want or like power. Again, the answer is a complete change of our society, returning to smaller, self-reliant and transparent units. A change, too, from an I-culture to a We-culture, or at least a bit more balanced between I and We. Let's all become 'aristoi'!

59. A group of Dutch Christians has published a cheap booklet popularising the ideas about a different, more frugal economy and a controlled, socially-responsible use of money. The booklet is useful for 'sensibilising' farmers, middle-sized entrepreneurs, trade unionists and the like.

60. Experiments are being conducted even to re-use our excrement – another soil nutrient that has been used for thousands of years. We now dump it in rivers and lakes and then try to remove it again by means of costly and inadequate purification plants. Our modern cleverness again!

Appendix 1
From Sandy Soils to the Sahel

Nature provides for all human requirements and our waste, in turn, forms raw material for nature. In former times, the land round villages provided us with food, and the manure (excrement) produced by our livestock and ourselves was returned to the land. As such, waste scarcely existed. The human population did, however, have to make an effort to ensure that natural limits were not exceeded. This was not always the case, though. If too much woodland was cleared, for instance, the water table dropped and the land tended to dry out. Limits were also exceeded if the soil was worked too intensively.

PRIMITIVE SETTLEMENT

In the Netherlands, the main problem was over-grazing or, more exactly, under-fertilisation. Livestock was allowed to graze so intensively, away from the village, that the vegetation was barely able to survive. The situation was aggravated by the introduction of the 'deep-litter' system, whereby livestock was brought back at night to sheds where manure accumulated in deep layers, subsequently to be transferred to the land around the village.

TRADITIONAL VILLAGE

The result was substantial impoverishment of pastures (grasslands) and a proportionate enrichment of the land around the village. This process of nutrient impoverishment and enrichment is at the expense of natural equilibria, and the probability of limits being exceeded is high. In the Netherlands, for instance, by the beginning of the present century sandy soils had developed from Groningen in the north to Limburg in the south. These sandy soils and sand drifts (small-scale deserts!) had once been rich pastures.

Throughout history, we see this process of over-development (nutrient-rich village soils) and under-development (nutrient-deficient sandy soils) continuing on an ever greater scale. As our numbers increased and our towns expanded, we required steadily larger areas of land to provide us with food and domestic fuel. Gradually, food and fuel had to be brought in from further afield and our waste materials became a problem.

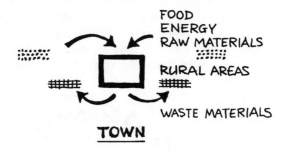

Our towns became 'enriched', in both senses of the word, at the expense of the rural areas. As the merchants, with their private capital, themselves began to produce for the market, agricultural practice was 'streamlined' on a large scale. The varied and decentralised system of cattle raising and crop cultivation began to make way for such monocultures as sheep farming (wool), flax cultivation (linen) and later market products, such as tulips. Many farmers were driven off their homelands and, robbed of their land, implements and a meaningful way of life, became the new urban proletariat. The class differences – a form of over- and under-development, but now in terms of human society – were thus reinforced. (The poverty situation, which the industrial revolution was to 'relieve' – thanks to the surplus of cheap labour that had become available, it might be added – was therefore not a normal state of affairs, but the result of the prior destruction of a reasonably healthy, labour-intensive economic infrastructure by the rise of the new, commercial, market economy.)

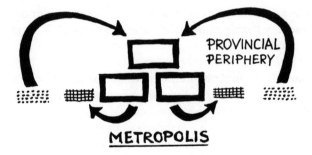

In the next phase, we see entire regions over-developing relative to more distant areas, e.g. the Dutch coastal conurbation relative to the rest of the country, Paris and northern France relative to Languedoc and Corsica. Today, the scale of this process has extended to encompass the entire globe, and we see rich, over-developed countries and even continents in vivid contrast with impoverished, under-developed countries and continents. The sand drifts of the Dutch province have become the Sahel, and Rotterdam's Europoort a latter-day 'deep-litter cowshed'.

The two poles are the result of one and the same process. The very last way to solve the problem, therefore, is to continue along the path of over-development in the affluent countries; neither is it to encourage the poor nations of the world to join the bandwagon of 'progress', i.e. western consumer society. From a point of view of energy consumption and natural resources (natural carrying capacity of the earth, environmental impact) such a policy is absolutely unfeasible, suicidal even. The 'north' should decrease its production over-

kill, to relieve the pressure on the rest of the world and on the global ecosystem
– and thus preserve the basic preconditions for a healthy global economy.

(Extract from "Groen in de buurt", Institute of Environmental Education,
Utrecht, 1985. Idea by Pieter Schroevers, based on the circles of the 19th
century economist Von Thünen.)

Appendix 2
Outlines of the Nineties

Contribution by Derk van Cappellen, Head of Future Studies, NOVACHEM Inc., to the NOVIB conference on 'Ecological survival – a South-North confrontation', Amsterdam, 11th and 12th October 1989.

Thank you, Mr. Chairman, for letting me have the microphone for a few minutes, as representative of T-5. T-5 stands for Think Tank of Twenty Top Transnationals. Its members, appointed by our boards of directors, ought to have an IQ of over 150 – a criterion by the way which we ourselves consider rather old fashioned.

Mr Khor from Malaysia has just mentioned the enormous flow of money going from the South to the North, as a result of the debts of the developing countries, and its devastating effects on their potential for development. Well, he will be pleased to hear that we too consider that policy as backward and that we are going to reverse that flow. We are going to provide the Third World with vast amounts of capital in order to help them once and for all to overcome their poverty and to – I dare say – civilise them, bring wealth to them as we have done most successfully during the last century to the working class, to the masses in our own, now rich countries.

Various speakers have put forward that only a quarter of the world population, mainly located in the North, uses over 80% of the world's resources. I am afraid I must correct this viewpoint, heard all too often. One forgets that the North produces for the whole world. Most of the advanced products and machinery in the Third World have been and are being produced in the North. It is the North that has taken upon itself the burden of manufacturing the bulk of the world's wealth – the same North having therefore to cope with the accompanying pollution and other unfavourable effects, the same North therefore being obliged to consume a considerable amount of the world's energy and commodities.

Another dubious presentation of facts concerns the difference between rich and poor countries. On the one hand, rates of income per capita or G.N.P.'s are given for the underdeveloped countries, intended to show the enormous gap with respect to the rich countries. Whereas on the other hand – often in the same paper or lecture – it is pointed out that many economic activities in the poorer countries are not counted, remain outside the financially recorded market. *My* conclusion would be that, in that case, the gap is apparently less wide than presented earlier. But this kind of sense does not always seem to be appreciated. Don't get me wrong, the gap often remains intolerably wide, but my point aims at a more correct approach of the facts.

Some people do not think positively about our sort of companies. They forget that the kinds of systems we have developed are the only ones capable of meeting the ever increasing needs of ever increasing numbers of people, while at the same time ensuring work for many people and income for the States, directly and via taxation of our shareholders. Only such accumulations of capital, equipment, technology and organisational know-how as we have are capable of meeting the challenges now facing us, most prominently combatting hunger, poverty and pollution.

For this reason, production must go on, products must be sold and this in turn requires purchasing power, i.e. consumers with money. Hence our intention to pump money into the Third World. This operation boils down to a simple widening of the money circulation, similar to, as I have said, what the progressive forces around 1900 undertook with the working classes in our own countries – to their general satisfaction, as you see in these countries where everyone now embraces the capitalist organisation of the economy, not in the least the socialist parties and the workers unions. And this example is, as we read daily in the newspapers, at last being followed all over the world where socialist deviations have been tried out.

We from T-5 have classified the environmental issue as a top priority. Henceforth we will help in banning such components as CFC's from our sprays and refrigerators. Our walkmen will have rechargeable batteries, our cokes will be distributed in returnable bottles, our cars will be equipped with catalytic converters, our fuels and detergents will spare the environment. Of course, there still remain a few problems to be overcome as regards the supply of energy and materials and waste disposal, but we are confident our technological capacity is able to handle these comfortably. While severely cutting the energy input, we reckon we can produce more while using less materials and producing less waste.

We will help in financing environmental education. If more consumers wish to buy 'green' products, we will be only too happy to produce them. The free market enables us to serve the consumer quickly and completely. Changing patterns and demands are the challenges we are geared to meet.

As for nature protection, we intend to help set up huge reserves in Asia, Africa and South America, sized so as to shelter not only pandas, rhinos and jaguars but also a number of original human tribes. Aren't they our fellow-hu-

mans from which we can learn valuable basic ecological principles and attitudes we so badly need nowadays? De-desertification and reforestation will
become two of our main activities, new wood one of our pilot products.

Our social mission we also consider of prime importance. The wealth we
spread, and will increasingly spread, includes, as you can see in the rich
countries, good housing, good education, good health care and birth control,
as well as mobility, recreation and culture. We also consider participation and
democracy as a necessary complement to our social-capitalism, as we say.
People should be free to refuse our products, they should control us, correct
us when need be, impose on us restrictions and taxes and be free to keep us
out of their country. (If you wish to see the effects of the last possibility, you
should hurry up and visit Albania and Cuba before they too change track...)

We are honest. We do not pretend to be able to raise the standard of living
of all the masses in the Third World which have often grown to sizes which
cannot possibly be served. We will start to do this for a fair proportion of the
population, enough to enable the country to make a definite switch to modern
capitalism and to stay free from oppositions and revolts which will put back
the clock of progress. As in the rich countries, a country needs some labour
reserve and differences in income in order to keep wages at a competitive level
and to dispose of savings for continuous investments.

Transnationalism, continued, sustainable growth (Green Growth, as we
say in T-5) and citizens' participation – these are also the key notions and action
lines of the Brundtland report. They can only be furthered by internationally
structured 'people's capitalism' as has long been promoted in the USA and is
now being developed in the European countries and most explicitly by the
Thatcher government currently privatising state owned companies. And isn't
this amazingly close to the idea of old Karl Marx about the people becoming
the owners of the means of production?

The distinguished guest from Malaysia quite rightly said it is not the
deterioration of the environment which has caused poverty but the other way
round. Well, let us therefore fight poverty first and accelerate economic
growth while developing the tools and structures necessary for ecological
sustainability. Let us, in a nature-saving way, produce and spread more of our
wealth, so that our brothers and sisters in the Third World can at last enjoy
similar wealth.

Thank you, Mr. Chairman.

T - 5

C/O A.A.R.D.E.

P.O.Box 533

3500 AM Utrecht

Netherlands

Ill. Arend van Dam

Literature

Aristotle, *The Politics*. Penguin Classics.

Binswanger, Hans, e.a. *Arbeit ohne Umweltzerstörung*. Fischer Perspektiven, 1988

Brundtland, Gro e.a. *Our Common Future*, U.N. report, 1987

Brown, Lester e.a. *State of the World - 1990*, Norton & Co, New York and London. (For criticism of the World Watch Institute: Sachs, Wolfgang: *The Virtue of Enoughness*, New Perspectives Quarterly, Spring 1989)

Burger, Willem, *Natural resource constraints, unemployment and government incentives for technical innovation*. In: Development and Peace, Vol. 6, No. 2, Autumn 1985

Childs, Marquis, *The Middle Way* (corrected by a new book, it seems).

Court, Thijs de la, *Beyond Brundtland*, Zed Books, London, 1990

Daly, Herman, e.a.(Hardin, Boulding, Georgescu-Roegen, quotations John Stuart Mill), *Economics, Ecology and Ethics*. Freeman & Co, New York, 1973 and 1980.

Ekins, Paul (Editor), *The Living Economy - A New Economics in the Making*. Routledge & Kegan Paul, London & New York, 1986 (Collection of papers from The Other Economic Summit.)

Galbraith, John K., *Russia needs more market, the West more state*. Article in: The Guardian, December 1989. *Money - whence it came, where it went*. Pelican, 1975. *A Short History of Financial Euphoria*. Whittle Direct Books.

George, Susan, *A Fate Worse than Debt*, Penguin Books, 1989

Goldsmith, Edward, *Blueprint for Survival*, Penguin 1972. *The Stable Society, Towards a social cybernatics*, Wadebridge Press, U.K., 1978. *The Great U-Turn*, Green Books, London, 1988

Gorz, André, *Ecologie et politique* (Galilée Paris, 1975) and *Ecologie et liberté* (id. 1977) In English: *Ecology and Politics*. Pluto Press, London.

Harle, Nigel, *Notes on Global Urgency*, Borderlands, Sittard, 1988.

Henderson, Hazel, *The Politics of the Solar Age: Alternative to Economics*. Doubleday, New York, 1980. *Creating Alternative Future - The End of Economics*. Perigee Books, New York, 1980

Hoogendijk, Willem, *Utopics - catalogus van alternatieven*, De Kargadoor,

194   The Economic Revolution

Utrecht, 1980. *De grote aandrijver,* Aktie Strohalm, Utrecht, 1980. *Hoe de zalm terug kwam,* Stichting Milieu-Educatie, Utrecht, 1988.

Hueting, Roefie, *New Scarcity and Economic Growth: more welfare through less production?* CBS, The Hague, 1980. *Energy, the Environment and Employment: a New Scenario.* In: Futures, Vol. 19, No. 3, June 1987.

Illich, Ivan, *Tools for Conviviality,* Harper & Row 1973.

Jänicke, Martin, *Wie das Industriesystem von seinen Misstanden profitiert.* Wiesbaden, 1979

Jungk, Robert, *51 Modelle für die Zukunft - Katalogus der Hoffnung,* Luchterhand Literaturverlag, Frankfurt a.M., 1990

Kropotkin, Peter, *Fields, factories and workshops tomorrow.* (1898!) George Allen & Unwin, London, 1974

Maruyama, Makoto, *Money and Substantive Economy: a study of Karl Polanyi's social and economic theory.* Paper York University, Toronto and Meiji Gakuin University, Yokohama, 1988

Morris, William, *News from Nowhere,* Penguin

Opschoor, Johannes B., *Economic Instruments for Environmental Protection,* OECD, Paris, 1989. *Economic Instruments for Sustainable Development,* Free University Amsterdam, 1990

Pearce, David e.a., *Blueprint for a Green Economy,* Earthscan Publications, London, 1989

Potma, Theo, *A Strategy for Change,* Centre for Energy-saving, Delft, 1990 (Paper)

Porritt, Jonathon, *Where on Earth are we going?* BBC, 1990

Sachs, Wolfgang: see under Brown, Lester

Suhr, Dieter, *The Capitalistic Cost-Benefit Structure of Money - An analysis of Money's Structural Non-neutrality and its Effects on the Economy.* Springer Verlag, 1989

Ullrich, Otto, *Weltniveau,* 1979

Vandana Shiva, *Development - The New Colonialism,* in: Development, Journal of SID, December 1989

Wachtel, Howard M.: *The Money Mandarins - The Making of a New Supranational Economic Order,* Pantheon Books, New York, 1986

Weizsäcker, E.U. von, *Erdpolitik - Oekologische Realpolitik an der Schwelle zum Jahrhundert der Umwelt.* Wissenschaftliche Buchgesellschaft, Darmstadt. 1989

Caring for the World, A strategy for sustainability, IUCN, UNEP and WWF, June 1990.

Concern for Tomorrow - A national environmental survey 1985 - 2010. National Institute of Public Health and Environmental Protection, Bilthoven, Netherlands, 1989

Le projet des Maires rureaux: Pour une France à villages humains. SIDER, 38 avenue Niel, 75017 Paris

The Ecologist (one of the world's best environmental magazines, based on both deep ecology and social justice. W.H.), Worthyvale Manor, Camelford, Cornwall, UK.

RECOMMENDED ESPECIALLY:

Hans Chr. Binswanger, *Geld und Natur - Die Dynamik der Geldwirtschaft*, Edition Weitbrecht, Thienemanns Verlag, Stuttgart, To be published in the course of 1991.

James Robertson, *Future Wealth - A New Economics for the 21st Century*. Cassell, U.K., 1990

Herman Daly and John Cobb Jr., *For the Common Good - Redirecting the Economy towards Community, Environment and a Sustainable Future*. Beacon Press, Boston, 1989 and Green Print, London, 1990

(N.B. The account of Daly's ideas in the book you now hold is based on his earlier book, above (1980). In some of the notes, however, reference is made to his later book, written with Cobb, which I have not yet had time to read in full. W.H.)

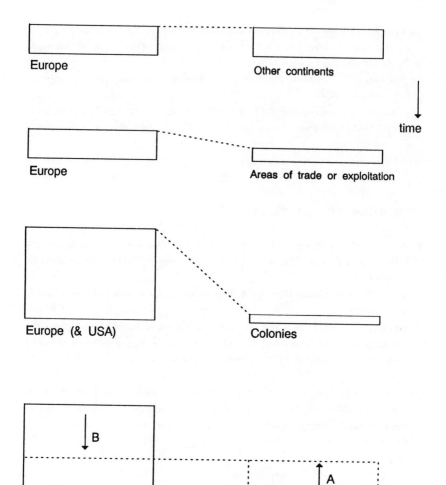

The history of the global welfare balance

A can only be achieved by means of B.

Why B is also necessary for the rich countries themselves (the 'North') is shown on page 142.

About the Author

After studying law (Leiden and Amsterdam), political science and art history (Paris), as well as working in a fine art gallery, Willem Hoogendijk joined the Council of Europe in Strasbourg. For 6 years he worked for its Council for Cultural Co-operation and specialised in educational radio and television.

Back in Holland, he worked for a short time in a factory ("some people go to Peru or Nepal, my unknown territory was the conveyor belt...") before joining the staff of an experimental youth and adult education centre in Utrecht (1970-1980).

Together with biologists, students and teachers, he started in 1970 the environmental pressure group Aktie Strohalm. From the outset, this group approached the environmental issue as a societal and economic problem, contrary to the mainstream idea that the root cause was people's state of mind and behaviour. Right from the start, the group's principal concerns were: economic growth, nuclear energy and energy policies, entropy, over- and under-development, green consumerism, water pollution, alternatives, people's participation. The motto was: 'Politicise the environmental movement, ecologise the political world.'

In 1975 he co-founded the Institute of Environmental Education, where he worked as a volunteer for 5 years until he could join its co-ordinating team as a paid worker in 1980. At present he helps the Institute, which now has a staff of 25, as one of its policy-makers.

His work on the money system has to be done in his spare time because it is not directly educational and, moreover, controversial.

The author is a co-founder of the Dutch Association for the Integrity of Creation and a participant in the Critical Farmers' Platform, in the National Environmental Platform and the Alliance for Sustainable Development. He is an adviser to the National Council of Refuse Collectors (of the Union of Civil Servants). He is also a member of the Council for the Environment of Utrecht city and of the Steering Committee of the European ecological group ECORO-PA.

About this book: "I had read that, some time ago, the Dutch 'green' economist Roefie Hueting ('My problem is that I say things which are too simple for learned people') met his colleague Herman Daly in Washington.

'Read anything new the last few years? I haven't,' Hueting said. 'No, neither have I,' answered Daly. Well, I hope this book contains a few novelties even for them, at last!"

Index

The cartoon was drawn by Scott Willis of the *San Jose Mercury News*.

SOME TERMS AND SUBJECTS

About 'Geld und Natur' by Hans Binswanger
(Addition to the second printing of the first edition)

The book by the Swiss professor of economics Hans Binswanger was not yet available when this book was being published. Some of its major points:
- In the mercantilistic view (Locke and others, second half of the 17th century) money was steering and pushing. However, this view was overruled by the classical (Hume, Smith) and neo-classical (Walras) theories, which regard money as merely following what is happening in the 'real' economy (as opposed to the realm of finance).
- However, while the theory became classical, the practice remained mercantilistic, viz. the credit system through the injection of (paper) money created by the state and the banks in Paris and, more succesfully by John Law, with the Bank of England. The neo-classical theory is 'draped' over economic reality, making it all but invisible, however, and the money system has been catapulted way out of the economic debate. (The well-known economist Joseph Schumpeter, too, had observed that the neo-classical school studies a capitalism deprived of its fundamental aspects. WH)
- With some exaggeration, B. states, one can identify as the essence of money its propensity to increase. The modern system of credit, creating money out of the blue, has realised the old dream of the alchemists to make gold: in the modern economy, alchemy lives on by other means.
- Surplus production became a necessary component to service the financial investors. Not only entrepreneurs but also investors are compelled to grow. Even just stabilisation on the income side will lead to a loss on the capital side. Investors, therefore, count on making a profit in order to avoid losing money. Hence a compulsion to growth.
- The master trick of the money economy (B. uses Hegel's term 'List der Vernunft') is the injection, in society, of (credit) money, prior to the production to be undertaken with that money, thus already generating the demand which the still-to-be-produced goods or services are yet to meet!
- Some of our production has to shrink, and this will unavoidably lead to a general shrinking of the economy. If we prefer a soft landing to a crash, we should lower the rate of interest and introduce a general system of ecotaxing. The resulting technological switch will lead us to qualitative growth.
- If this does not work, or not fast enough, we will have to reconsider the whole system of financing, with its inherent dynamism and compulsion to growth. This operation may be necessary in any case in view of the worrying instability of the modern, international system of money and financing. Such a revision should also encompass corporate law, the functioning of the financial markets and the sphere of influence of money.

The above is a brief account of two chapters of Binswanger's important pioneering book, the value of which lies in its combining a historical account with an analysis of current practice. May it open the minds of his colleagues!

Errata & additions

(Addition to the second printing of the first edition)

p. 26 Most economist argue: "In a market, goods have a price: the scarcer, the dearer. So it is with money, too." So far, nothing apparently abnormal.

p. 29 Legend: Stock exchange or purse! (in French: bourse).

p. 38 The term 'neg-entropy' is controversial, since there is always some entropy. More precisely: 'low entropy'.

p. 45 In a second edition I will devote more space to Mill and also consider the physiocrats. Binswanger explains how the old cooperation between labour and nature has gradually been replaced by that between labour and capital. The focus on human labour has reduced our awareness of nature's 'labour', while the growing importance of (endless) money has closed our eyes to nature's limits. Nature has in fact simply been reduced to land and raw materials.

p. 57 Needs c: needs for repairing **or preventing** damage.
Needs d: another example is the accelerated need to renew machines because of the fierceness of competition.

p. 59 As regards our desires, many, of course, are not 'pushed' by money. On the other hand, without money wishes remain dreams. Only through the availability of money (savings, the possibility of a loan) are dreams turned into realizable desires. When money is not actually pushing, it is at least seducing! See how keen banks are to offer loans!

p. 71 Money cloud: is this the manifestation of another way for money to be diverted away from being reinvested directly in the 'real economy', i.e. by buying other money (and bonds and other financial values)? This may be done to prevent too much money flowing into the real economy, which would result in money becoming too cheap. Money buying money means less pressure on the real economy – a piece of luck in the overall mishap?

p. 84 As regards the taming of money, I tentatively advanced such measures as an eco-steered rate of interest and less mobile capital. I also think the institution of **bank credit** ought to be reconsidered. It stimulates economic activities without us having to make any previous sacrifice (savings or stopping other activities): very unecological and therefore suicidal!

p. 91 The proposed flexibilisation is illustrated on p. 162. Not automatically withdrawing investments in the case of lower remuneration would mean a reduced mobility of capital. See also note 38. (How much would this infringe upon the free market? Or should we distinguish between the financial market and the market of goods and services (the real economy) and would it, therefore, mean some 'liberation' of the second from the pressure the first?)

p. 92   The seesaws should be interchanged.

p. 103   It is the necessity of ecological survival which will bind us together!

p. 109   The British economist A.C. Pigou should be mentioned in connection with ecotaxing, since he was the first to suggest internalizing the external costs of a commodity in its price. 'True' pricing would, among other things, upset the entire worldwide division of labour, which is now based on 'comparative advantages' (Ricardo) calculated by means of too short yardsticks. Just consider the full energy costs of transport and mono-production, with their attendant loss of diversity of production everywhere.

p. 113   The illustration refers to the distribution of wealth, whereas the legend refers to a second way of diminishing the influence of the state, viz. by internalising costs.

p. 123   What we should also do (another dot) is reconsider the creation of money by banks, because (a) it considerably increases the volume of money and (b) it is directed by very short yardsticks (i.e. the short-term return). Moreover, these yardsticks are private, which may also be of disadvantage to society.

p. 130   The sentence 'The group...' (line 8 from bottom) should be placed 9 lines up, after the litter-clean-up day.

p. 135   The community panels, created by USA companies, are called Public Advisory Panels.

p. 162   The illustration applies to Flexibilisation on p. 91.

p. 163   Line 23: ...system, **a never satisfied creator of needs.**

p. 174   Note 34: A higher interest rate results, as we know, in less risk investments and therefore in lower productivity. There is a tension between savings/investments and consumptin. Compared with Japan, the USA, for example, is said to consume too much.

p. 179   Line 13 from bottom: see not the following note, but note 44.

p. 180   Note 43: The interview was published 1-6-'89.

p. 193   Literature: important authors forgotten: Barry Commoner, Dennis Meadows (reports of the Club of Rome), A.C. Pigou, Joan Robinson, E.F. Schumacher (Small is beautiful) and Günther Schwab. Apologies!

p. 200   Galbraith, **John** Kenneth. Gorz, André: omit 176. Porritt.